A Saint
On Every
Corner

A Saint _{on} Every Corner

Glimpses of Holiness
Beyond the Monastery

Albert Holtz, O.S.B.

Illustrations by the author

AVE MARIA PRESS   Notre Dame, Indiana 46556

International Standard Book Number: 0-87793-639-0 (PB)

0-87793-640-4 (CB)

Cover and text design by Brian C. Conley

Printed and bound in the United States of America.

Library of Congress Cataloging-in-Publication Data

Holtz, Albert.
    A saint on every corner: glimpses of holiness beyond the monastery / Albert Holtz.
        p. cm.
    ISBN 0-87793-640-4 (hardcover). — ISBN 0-87793-639-0 (pbk.)
    1. Christian life—Meditations. 2. Holiness—Christianity
    —Meditations. 3. Christian life—Catholic authors.
    4. Holtz, Albert—Journeys.   I. Title.
BX2350.2.H587 1998
242—dc21   97-41439
                                                            CIP

To all the saints of
St. Joseph's Parish,
Maplewood, New Jersey

Paris: Sacré Coeur de Montmartre

Table of Contents

Introduction

The Dream

The monastery seems unusually peaceful this morning. A bright spring sun slants through the venetian blinds in warm yellow slices. I sit down in my rocking chair to steal fifteen minutes of quiet before I start another hectic workday at school. The morning traffic in downtown Newark murmurs in the distance like the swish of surf on a sandy shore. My eyelids get heavier and heavier . . .

I'm riding a swing in a tall oak tree. As I lean way back and push my feet out in front of me, I feel the swing gain speed. Suddenly the ropes come undone and tie themselves to the next higher bough. As I keep swinging, the ropes keep working themselves upward, climbing from branch to branch until finally the swing is attached to the very top of the tree. A wide blue sky stretches above me. Just over my head fireworks are bursting in fountains of colored sparkles. Thrilled by the feeling of openness and freedom, I whoop for joy at the top of my voice. With every new arc, the swing takes me higher until my toes are pointing almost straight over my head. I stretch and strain to touch the fireworks. I kick . . . stretch . . . kick . . . stretch . . . Still I can't quite reach. Kick . . . stretch . . .

Suddenly a gentle voice whispers:

"Albert, just let go!"

I ignore this bizarre suggestion and keep straining to touch the sparkles. Kick . . . stretch . . . kick . . .

Then the voice calls again, coaxing me:

"It's okay. Just let go and watch what happens!"

I hang on stubbornly and keep up my dogged struggle to reach the sky: Kick . . . stretch . . . kick . . .

I wake up with my heart pounding and both hands clutching the wooden arms of the rocking chair. The clock says 8:01—time to shake off my dream and get to class. Rubbing the sleep out of my eyes and smoothing the wrinkles out of my Benedictine habit, I stumble over to school.

A question nags me like a toothache on my way down the stairs: *What would have happened if I had actually let go?* The more I think about it, the more frustrated I get. "I should have just let go of that swing!" I decide, a little too late. *If I ever hear that voice again, though,* I promise myself, *I won't make the same mistake twice.* I arrive at class in a bad mood.

The Surprise

Some months pass. Every now and then, I relive my dream and wonder what might have happened if I had been less of a coward. Then one afternoon, I go to the Abbot's office to talk with him about my upcoming twenty-fifth anniversary of ordination to the priesthood. There's a custom in our monastery that on the occasion of such an anniversary a monk can go on a long vacation during the summer. As a French teacher I've enjoyed two summers in Europe studying French, so I'm hoping to do something like that again for my anniversary.

In the midst of our conversation, the Abbot looks at me and says, "You know, I just thought of something. Instead of going away just for the summer, what about taking a *whole year* instead? You know, away from the monastery, a break from the teaching, computer programming, and school administration." Starting to warm up to his own idea, he goes on, "You can just do anything you want: travel, study, whatever. It would do you a lot of good—in ways that neither of us can even imagine right now. What do you think?"

I'm caught totally off guard by the offer. On the other hand, though, I'm completely prepared for it: this is the voice on the swing challenging me again: "*Just let go and watch what happens!*" With no thought as to how I'll ever be able to survive outside the monastery for so long, or how the monastic community and the school will possibly survive without me, I answer right away, "Sure! I'd *love* that!"

So in the middle of that June, I pack some clothes and my habit along with a bible, a breviary, a sketch pad, and two blank journals. I say good-bye to my brother monks and receive the Abbot's blessing. Pausing at the monastery door, I glance back down the familiar hallway one last time. Then I take a deep breath, reach for the doorknob, and let go of the swing.

For eleven months I fly through the fireworks of fifteen countries. From Bavaria to Bolivia, from Amsterdam to Zamora, I soar. I hike in the snow-clad Swiss Alps, and I taste the warm mist of the jungle-girded Iguazu Falls in Brazil. I sing Vespers in Latin with cloistered nuns near Florence and celebrate New Year's Eve with a delightful group of college students in Szentes, a bleak town in Hungary's Great Plain. I sleep in monasteries, rectories, religious houses, and, a few times, in a family's home, but I travel alone, and so come to enjoy a close friendship with the God of pilgrims and exiles.

The Saints

In New Testament times all baptized Christians were called "saints." St. Paul uses the word in his epistles to refer to the members of the different communities to whom he writes. For centuries, baptized people continued to think of themselves as "the saints" (from the Latin *sanctus*, "holy"). Catholics have now come to use "saint" as an honorary title reserved for certain rare and extraordinary people who work miracles and lead lives of heroic holiness, but both the Second Vatican Council and the recent *Catechism of the Catholic Church* have reminded us that all Christians—married or single, lay people or religious—are called to one and the same holiness, to sainthood. The Church is the People of God, a holy people, a church of "saints."

In my travels I met many of the "official" saints, like Francis of Assisi and Thérèse of Lisieux. The ones that taught me the most, though, were the unheralded saints: folk dancers in Catalonia, kite-flyers in Normandy, and a catechist in rural Bolivia.

I visited many "official" holy places like Fátima, but there were also lessons for me in unofficial ones: the waterfront of the Spanish fishing port of Muros, a Paraguayan bus on the road to Asuncion, and a living room in Gödöllő, north of Budapest.

In every new place I visited, I discovered a new aspect of our call to holiness and a different dimension of God's constant, loving presence in the world.

The Stories

When I got home and started reading my travel journal, I realized that I had brought back with me, hidden between its covers, dozens of insights about holiness. Since they don't belong to me but to all the saints, I gladly share them with the reader of this book. Although the stories can be read in any order, they are grouped in six chapters according to certain themes.

The meditations in Part One deal with "The Gift of Imperfection." The saints in books always seem too perfect: they never feel a twinge of fear, never say a sharp word, and never lose their cool under pressure. The imperfect saints I met on my journey, though, helped me to see that imperfections are an important and even necessary part of God's plan to make us all holy.

Part Two, "Saints on My Street," assumes that ever since the Word became flesh, every place on earth is a holy place filled with God's saving presence, and that every human activity is a sacred activity. We are all destined to become saints, then, by living the particular life to which each of us has been called: parent, spouse, employee, student, and so forth. These five stories celebrate the sacredness that is found in the ordinary routine of our daily lives.

The stories in Part Three, "Holy Combat," teach us that although holiness is a gift and not something we earn, we still have to struggle to nurture and protect it. St. Peter warns the saints: "Keep sober and alert, because your enemy the devil is on the prowl . . ." (I Pet 5:8). The episodes in this section, then, reflect an ancient tradition: the spiritual life as a "sacred warfare" in which the enemy is the devil and the battlefield is the human heart.

Part Four, "Holiness 101," reminds us that God is constantly teaching us how to be holy. There are lessons for us in the most unlikely places if we know how to look, and in the most unlikely people if we know how to listen. An insight may come from something as quiet as a sunset in Saint Malo, or as exciting as a train ride through the Channel Tunnel.

In Part Five, "Saints in Action," we see people responding to Christ's call, "If you love me, then show me!" For them, love is not a feeling or an abstract state of mind, but an activity. They remind us that the one criterion by which we each will be judged is this: did you love?

The stories in the final part, "Saints With Open Arms," challenge us to a holy openness. The saint embraces everything about being human, finding God in the painful as well as in the pleasant. We are called to risk loving all people with God's own free, unbounded love, a love which knows no walls, no safe limits, and no fear.

I hope that these meditations may be of some value to my brothers and sisters on their road to holiness. This book is my inadequate way of saying thank you to all those saints who taught me so much the year I let go of the swing.

Kientzheim Alsace

Part One
The Gift of Imperfection

Saints With Cold Feet

Canterbury, England

Canterbury is lively and welcoming this November afternoon. Her streets, lined with pubs and souvenir shops, are noisy with the tongues of a dozen different lands. People still flock to visit the magnificent Gothic cathedral and its tomb of Thomas Becket, just as they've been doing since the late 1100s. Along these bustling lanes once walked the Wife of Bath, the bawdy Miller, the courtly Knight, the Pardoner, and other colorful pilgrims in Geoffrey Chaucer's *Canterbury Tales*, who told each other stories to pass the time on the road.

But if Canterbury breathes welcome and warmth, she also has an air of Saxon solidity, thanks to her cobblestone pavements, granite fences, moss-covered church walls, and grumpy gray ramparts of rough flint. Canterbury is a stony place.

I've left behind me her bustling streets and crowded pubs. Behind me, too, the towers of the cathedral and the ancient city walls. I'm off in search of a special spot that hides about a half-mile outside of town.

I turn left up a narrow road that climbs a wooded slope. After a few minutes, a tiny church peeks out from among the trees on the hilltop. This is Saint Martin's, the earliest place of continuous Christian worship in all of England. It was already ancient when Bede the Venerable wrote in the early 700s that it was "built of old while the Romans were still inhabiting Britain."

In the year 580, when Canterbury was the capital of the Kingdom of Kent, the pagan King Ethelbert married a Christian princess named Bertha. The Queen had an oratory on this spot, and it was here that Ethelbert, now converted to Christianity, was baptized in 598 by St. Augustine of Canterbury.

Near the crest of the hill I turn up a footpath that leads through the little churchyard, and stand for a while looking at the old building. Despite improvements made in the twelfth century, some of the outside walls still show original Roman brickwork.

I walk slowly into the dark, silent chapel, overwhelmed by the sense of holiness of this sacred place whose roots have tapped deep into the rocky Kentish soil since the time of the Romans. All alone in the silence, I sit on a wooden bench and let my imagination wander easily back over the centuries. . . .

Pope St. Gregory the Great has chosen Augustine, prior of a monastery in Rome, to lead a band of monks to evangelize this pagan territory of the Angles. Their vow of obedience and their missionary zeal speed the little band on their way, full of joy and enthusiasm. But as they travel overland through Gaul, they begin to hear disturbing tales of the savage and murderous English natives. There are graphic details of the strange customs and the unpronounceable tongue that await them. There are sailors' hair-raising reports of the treacherous currents and killer storms that lie in wait for travelers crossing the English Channel. The list of hazards gets longer every day. The missionaries' enthusiasm for their task evaporates like the morning mist, and finally they hold a meeting to discuss whether this mission is really such a good idea after all. Caution wins out: they send Augustine back to Rome to explain to Pope Gregory the impossibility of the task and ask papal permission to return to their monastery.

If Augustine and his little band get their way, the Saxons might have to remain in their pagan darkness for a few more centuries. But the Pope is insistent and sends Augustine right back to his companions with a letter of encouragement—and strict orders not to turn around again!

The monks obediently continue their journey to Britain and today are venerated as great pioneer saints. But it's nice to know that they, too, were subject to an occasional case of cold feet! Like the rest of us, they were susceptible at times to discouragement and doubt.

Saint Augustine of Canterbury and his holy monks give hope to me and to all would-be saints. Their lives, like mine, included fear as well as faith, defeats as well as victories, weaknesses as well as virtues. The Canterbury monks are the patron saints of people who get cold feet. In the dark vaults of Saint Martin's church, they whisper to me this afternoon that anyone really can become a saint by struggling faithfully every day with fears and doubts and hesitations.

I bid good-bye to the voices in the chapel and step outside into the chilly churchyard cemetery on the hilltop. Gray clouds still hang low over the roofs and towers of Canterbury below. The first raindrops begin to tap me gently on the shoulder, and I shiver in the November dampness as I turn to head back down to the bus station.

Unfinished Saints

Dieppe, France

The sturdy brick houses of this newer section of Dieppe, up in the hills east of the old town, are designed to keep out the damp and chill that are so typical of Normandy. As we drive to church this Sunday morning I say to my hosts, "Well, maybe there'll be some sun later today." I've been staying with Bernard and Colette for almost a week, and I'm still waiting for the first sunny ray to appear.

For me, the name Dieppe conjures up black-and-white images of smoldering ruins and beaches littered with charred invasion vehicles. In 1942, a Canadian force attempted a beach landing in German-occupied Normandy a couple of miles west of here. It cost a thousand lives, but the Allied commanders got what they'd hoped to get: knowledge about amphibious landings on the shores of Normandy. The lessons learned at Dieppe would pay off two years later during the historic "D-Day" invasion.

We arrive at the neighborhood church, where I am introduced to the pastor and invited to concelebrate the Sunday eucharist with him. As we wait for mass to start, my host shows me around his parish church. There's not a whole lot to see. It's a large brick structure, with pleasant rounded arches running down both sides of the central nave. As we're walking toward the sacristy, he points out the pillars that support the arches. "You see how the columns near the altar are perfectly smooth cylinders? Well, now look at the ones in the body of the church."

When I turn around and look out into the body of the church, I see what he's getting at: the rest of the pillars are different. They're not smooth, cylindrical columns but rather twelve-sided pillars, with a dozen flat facets running top to bottom.

"Some people say that the original plan was for all the columns to be rounded smoothly like the ones up front here, but they ran short of cash. So to save money they didn't round off the rest of the pillars but left them unfinished, with all those flat sides."

Time to get vested. In a few minutes I'm walking out into the sanctuary with the parish priest to celebrate Sunday mass. I can spot Bernard and Colette in the congregation. A few rows in front of them is the old gentleman who came by yesterday and spoke, over a glass of port, about the day the Canadians landed. Several African girls from a nearby boarding school are standing together on the other side of the aisle. We all sit down for the readings and the sermon.

I look out toward the crowded pews, and I notice those unfinished pillars—twelve-sided, incomplete. It occurs to me that this is an unfinished church. It will always be unfinished.

Then, as I look out at the faces in the congregation, I realize that we're all members of an unfinished Church. As the People of God we'll never be quite perfect—at least not this side of heaven. Ours will always be an incomplete Church—always striving toward perfection, and always falling short. Just like this parish church building, the Church on earth will never be finished.

The sermon is over, and we stand and pray a litany of intentions for various needs, the whole congregation responding "*Seigneur, exauce-nous*"—"Lord, hear our prayer." We sit again and sing an offertory hymn as two parishioners bring up the bread and the wine to be used on the altar.

The main reason that the Church is unfinished, of course, is that we human beings are perpetually unfinished ourselves. We've all experienced the sense that there is always something more to learn, to accomplish, to become. It is this "incurable unfinishedness," as one philosopher calls it, that sets us apart from other living things, because in trying to "finish" ourselves, we become creators. Our incurable unfinishedness keeps us childlike, capable of learning and growing. We're never perfect, though we may be trying to head in that direction.

I look again at one of the twelve-sided columns, and it occurs to me: imperfection is not only okay; it's our unique strong point. We're *supposed* to be unfinished! Humans exist in the gap between what is and what could be, between the reality and the dream, the already and the not-yet. And it is precisely in this gap that the saints are found. Virtue presumes that we are not yet at the ideal: virtue is the struggle to close the gap between what we are and what we're called to be—we can be virtuous, we can be saints, only if we're imperfect!

Prayer, in fact, is the spirit's response to the experience of the gap, of being "hungry for God." The psalmist prays in Psalm 42, "As a deer yearns for running streams, so I yearn for you, my God." I can only pray if I'm unfinished.

And if human beings are imperfect, then saints are, too. Imperfections, setbacks, and sins are all part of the striving; they're all grist for the mill. They're the place where we are destined to meet God—in the gap. Wherever there is that unfinishedness, there is the call to sainthood: in the kitchen, the office, the hospital room, or the supermarket. Wherever there is that sense of striving, there is a saint in the making. From this point of view, then, there is no such thing as an "obstacle" to sainthood. Saints can have short tempers, struggles with jealousy or greed, and preoccupations with raising a family and balancing the checkbook. Whether we're dealing with a too-crowded daily schedule, a character flaw, a painful experience in the past, a physical disability, no matter what, it is through and in the experience of our imperfections that God wants to meet us.

We stand now for the Eucharist Prayer, the most solemn part of the mass. The church is filled with the melody of the *"Saint! Saint! Saint!"*—"Holy! Holy! Holy!" I look out at the people singing. Here are saints, with cares and trials, problems and sins, shortcomings and fears. Here is the Church.

A bright ray of light pours through a window to my left. The sun at last! It highlights a twelve-sided pillar, one of those unfinished columns in an unfinished church filled with unfinished saints.

coimbra – Portugal

Saint Material

Fátima, Portugal

The train south from Coimbra, Portugal, to Fátima is a real "local," calling at every little village. We arrive fifty-five minutes late at the station marked "Fátima." That's when I find out that the railroad station is called "Fátima" not because it's located in or anywhere near the town of that name, but because it's as close as the train gets. I soon learn that I still have another twenty-some miles to go, and that the only practical way is by taxi for the flat rate of $20 one-way.

The ride along winding roads through the rugged mountain country of central Portugal finally brings me to the real Fátima, and the taxi drops me off near an entrance at one side of the great sanctuary. A short walk between two large buildings brings me out into a scene that is awash with warm spring sunlight. The basilica, begun in 1928, extends its huge semicircular porticoes like welcoming arms to embrace Mary's visitors who come to her shrine from all parts of the world. The wide expanse of empty pavement spreads downhill like a great gray meadow, waiting for the return of the huge throngs of summer.

Today, respectful pilgrims are sprinkled in small handfuls around the plaza, strolling slowly in different directions as they enjoy the first real taste of spring. The atmosphere is serene—there is an unmistakable air of prayerfulness and peace.

On the immense plaza, off to the left as I face the basilica, stands a modern concrete-and-glass canopy, open on the sides. I walk in under the roof and sit on one of the wooden pews arranged in a horseshoe around a sanctuary. Inside the rails of the sanctuary stands a short pillar of white marble that supports a statue of Our Lady of Fátima. This is the real hub of Fátima, the focal point for four million visitors a year, because it marks the exact location of the bush on which stood the "lady more brilliant than the sun" that May afternoon in 1917. The little bush has long ago been reverently pulled to pieces by eager hands.

As the miraculous appearances continued through the summer of 1917, more and more people came to wait with little ten-year-old Lucia and her cousins, Francisco and Jacinta. At the final apparition, on October 13, 1917, about 70,000 people were here in the Cova da Iria to see what would happen. The Lady appeared as promised, and told the children that she was "The Lady of the Rosary." She asked that a chapel be built here in her honor. At the end of the apparition, everyone present saw the miracle that Our Lady had promised the children: "the sun, resembling a silver disc, could be gazed at without difficulty and, whirling on itself like a wheel of fire, it seemed about to fall upon the earth."

Well, those first visitors are gone, and of the three children only Lucia, now a Carmelite nun in a convent in Coimbra, is still alive. The meadow of the Cova da Iria has changed beyond recognition. But behind the large canopy where I'm sitting, you can still see the oak tree under which the children used to pray the rosary while waiting for the promised appearances on the thirteenth of each month. The other authentic reminder of the great events of 1917 stands in front of me in the sanctuary, a few feet behind the statue. It is a little country chapel, a tiny oratory that looks as if it might seat about eighteen people. The Lady had commanded that a church be built here in her honor, and this white chapel was the answer to her request.

A constant stream of visitors flows in and out under the canopy. Parents with tiny children in tow come to pray the rosary; a few older people, stooped under the weight of cares and years, just sit in quiet meditation. I've got plenty of company as I pray a rosary for my long list of relatives and friends.

I sit gazing at the whitewashed chapel. It *is* awfully modest. Could this possibly be what Mary had in mind when she asked that a church be built in her honor? They must have misunderstood. She must have meant "build me a magnificent basilica glowing with gold and precious stones."

A whole busload of pilgrims from Italy surges in to kneel near the statue in front of the chapel, but the silence remains unbroken. I start to pray the First Joyful Mystery of the rosary, the Annunciation, meditating on the scene of Mary being asked to become the mother of the Messiah, to carry the Son of God in her womb. I think of St. Paul's prayer in his Letter to the Ephesians, "that Christ may live in your hearts through faith." Each of us is supposed to be a saint, a holy sanctuary, an abode of the Divine. A leaflet on the bench in front of me catches my eye. Along the bottom in large type are the English words, "Build me a church!" I wonder if God doesn't ask the same of each of us: "Make your life into a dwelling place for me."

Immediately, I start mumbling excuses, trying to get out of the assignment: I have nothing to build with . . . I don't possess any heroic virtues or remarkable talents. In fact, I have a few pretty glaring faults. I can't build a basilica with what I've got— look at me! All I could bring to the project would be things like my short temper, my big ego, and my distractions at prayer. Imperfections and struggles aren't good enough materials for building a dwelling place for God.

I look up and gaze more closely at the simple chapel in front of me, the first one built in response to Our Lady's request for a church. It's hardly a church compared with the great buildings I've seen in my travels. It's actually just one of those humble, rustic oratories you find all over the European countryside.

But then, Mary of Nazareth was a country girl from a small village herself. When she asked the poor farmers around the Cova da Iria to make her a church, she must have known that they couldn't afford anything big or showy, no stained glass or Italian marble. The local people understood her perfectly and they built her church with what they had at hand—local stone, wood from the forest, and sand from the river. What I'm looking at here is *exactly* what Our Lady of Fátima had in mind.

In my own struggle to become a sanctuary for God to dwell in, the plain white chapel of Fátima's farmers has a comforting message for me: you build your church with what you've got! You don't mourn the fact that you have no marble or silver or stained glass. You give God what you have, the life you're able to lead, with its limitations and failings. You pray even though you have distractions, you raise your children even if you're sometimes impatient with them, and you offer God your daily work even if it can't always be done as well as you'd like it to be.

The last bead of my rosary slides between my fingers. The end of the Fifth Joyful Mystery, the Finding of Jesus in the Temple. I look at my watch and realize that it's almost time to find a taxi for the return ride to the station. I take one last look at the chapel, then walk out into the spring sunshine and cross in front of the great basilica with its impressive colonnades.

By eight o'clock, I'll be back in Coimbra, the town where Lucia de Jesus, the ten-year old Lucia of 1917, still lives in the Carmelite convent. I bet I can guess which of these two churches is her favorite.

The Saint Who Lost His Cool
Ligugé, France

I'm passing through the fertile farmlands of France's Poitou region on the train from Paris to Bordeaux. We're about five minutes south of Poitiers when I look out the window to my left. The narrow, tree-lined canal that lies lazily alongside the tracks was built by the Romans when this was the province of Gallia. I quickly look out the other side of the train in time to glimpse a collection of stone buildings huddling around a church tower. This is the Benedictine Abbey of Ligugé, said to be the oldest monastery in the Western Christian world. Its story takes me on a trip back in time . . .

About the year A.D. 361, a strange young man in his late twenties took up residence in the ruins of an ancient Gallo-Roman villa on the site of the present monastery. He was born in Pannonia (present-day Hungary) but was raised in Italy. At the age of fifteen, he had been forced by law to follow in the footsteps of his father, who was an officer in the Roman army. Three years later, he was baptized a Christian and soon became a disciple of Hilary, the saintly bishop of nearby Poitiers.

Well-known for his holiness of life even before his baptism, over time the young man will become more and more famous for the countless miraculous cures he performs. As so often happens to holy men in the fourth century, he will eventually be drafted by the people to become bishop of their town.

As bishop of Tours, he will become an energetic foe of the pagan cults that still flourish in the Roman Empire at the time. His fame as a miracle worker will spread across Gaul, and by the time of his death he will already be honored as "Saint Martin of Tours." Many paintings and statues recall the famous story of his cutting his soldier's cloak down the middle in order to give half of it to a beggar. The next night, the story goes, Jesus appeared to him clothed in the cloak he'd given to the poor man.

In the earliest *Life of Saint Martin*, Sulpicius Severus gives a long and impressive list of the monk-bishop's wonderful deeds to prove that Martin was a perfect saint whom God always protected from all harm. After the *Life* was published, however,

Sulpicius felt he had to write a letter to a certain Eusebius to defend Martin from slander: There was a story spreading of how the supposedly invulnerable Martin had once been burned in a fire. Here is the story that Sulpicius retells.

Martin is making the rounds of the parishes in his diocese and decides to sleep in a little room attached to the church he is visiting. He is uncomfortable with the luxury of the straw mattress that has been made up for him and so pushes the straw aside and sleeps on the wooden floor. During the night, a defective stove used for heating the room sets fire to the straw and Martin is awakened around midnight by a cloud of thick, choking smoke. He gropes his way quickly to the door and begins pulling frantically on the bolt to unlock it. The bolt won't budge! Within a few moments, the flames fill the room and engulf the bishop, singeing the hem of his robe. Weak with fear, he struggles again with the stubborn bolt. Still no luck! Let's let Sulpicius finish the story in his own flowery style:

> At length recovering his habitual conviction that safety lay not in flight but in the Lord, and seizing the shield of faith and prayer, committing himself entirely to the Lord, he lay down in the midst of the flames. Then indeed, the fire having been removed by divine intervention, he continued to pray amid a circle of flames that did him no harm.

By Martin's own admission, he had taken longer than he should have to turn to the power of prayer. He'd been startled out of a sound sleep to find himself in terrible danger. The saint later spoke of this incident as a snare that the devil had laid for him, a snare that, for a moment, had worked.

Sulpicius is truly indignant when people imply that this scene shows some imperfection in Martin. "This event which is ascribed to the infirmity of Martin," he says, "is, in reality, full of dignity and glory, since indeed, being tried by a most dangerous calamity, he came forth a conqueror."

The story certainly does end in dignity and glory, but maybe Christians would be better served by meditating on what the good bishop did for the first half-minute after he smelled smoke. I keep hoping to find a painting of this scene: Saint Martin, eyes wide with fright, desperately tugging with both hands at the rusty bolt as flames lick at his robe. *That* is a saint I could identify with.

I've experienced that minute of panic many times, when I've forgotten that God is there with me. I've been in the flames of difficult situations when everything seems to be coming apart and it takes me too long to hand things over to the Lord. There have been times when I, like Saint Martin, the great Bishop of Tours, have wasted time tugging at the rusty bolt and only later remembered to stop trying to control things and turn confidently to the power of prayer.

Maybe I could settle for a picture of the saint lying in prayer on the burning floor, untouched by the flames all around him. In any case, Martin of Tours is the one I pray to for the grace to keep my cool when I'm starting to panic. He knows what that feeling is like.

The blur of gray buildings is well behind us now, and the train continues rattling southwest toward the sea. No one else is looking out the window.

A Church of Sinners

Santa Cruz, Bolivia

In the open-air market, I've seen the dried llama fetuses that one buries in the foundation of a new house to ward off evil. In the center of town, I've marveled at the old women who sit on the sidewalk patiently waiting all day for someone to buy one or two of the oranges they've put on the blanket in front of them. On my long walks from the rectory here in Santa Cruz, in the semi-tropical center of Bolivia, I've watched shiny new Porsches dodge around burro-powered carts on the highway. A few days ago, on Palm Sunday, I saw little children sitting at the gate of the church-yard selling palms before mass. Nothing surprises me anymore now that I've been here for over a week.

So I'm not surprised when a woman shows up for the Good Friday service car-rying a long ribbon-like piece of last Sunday's palm. Then, as people start filling the pews, I notice more and more of these yellow branches appearing. By the time the service starts in honor of the Passion and Death of Our Lord, there are palms in ev-ery part of the church.

The service begins in silence with the altar servers leading the procession. The priests quietly prostrate themselves on the floor of the sanctuary for a moment as a sign of repentance. Then we all stand and the pastor prays the opening oration. Ev-eryone sits down and the readings begin.

In the deep faith of the *campesinos*, the simple country people, religious practices are sometimes a confused mixture of native religion, superstition, and imperfect Christian theology. But when I look out over the crowded church this Good Friday afternoon, their custom of celebrating "Palm Friday" starts to speak powerfully to me. The pious folks who have come back today carrying last Sunday's palms with them actually show deep insight into the great paradox of Christian life.

The bright yellow strips of palm are accusing fingers pointing to a sad truth: we are the same people who greeted Jesus at his triumphal entrance into Jerusalem just last Sunday. We recognized the Messiah and sang out in joy, "Hosanna to the Son of

David! Blessed is he who is coming in the name of the Lord!" We tore branches off of trees and laid them on the road for his donkey to walk on. But that was Sunday. And this is Friday. Today our hands, the same hands that waved the branches in homage, are clenched fists shaking angrily at the pathetic figure crowned with thorns. The same congregation that was Sunday's welcoming throng has turned into Friday's bloodthirsty mob. The same voices that sang out "Hosanna! Hosanna!" last Sunday are shouting "Crucify him! Crucify him!" this afternoon.

After the readings and prayers comes the ceremony of the veneration of the cross. Worshippers stream single-file toward the crucifix to kiss the image of their Savior. Once again, the accusing palms appear here and there in the line.

We are amazingly fickle creatures when you think about it. We pray, we go to church, and then without a qualm we turn and calmly crucify Christ in our neighbor with a well-aimed insult. We thank God with great fervor for loving us unconditionally, but then a moment later refuse to help a neighbor in need. Palm Sunday turns into Good Friday with alarming speed.

At the end of the service, a procession forms behind a life-size cross that is being carried out of the church and through the streets on a public Way of the Cross. The church empties as the crowd starts on its way to visit fourteen stations that have been placed around the neighborhood. Once again, several yellow palms lift their sharp points upward, looking more and more like accusing fingers all the time as they wave slowly in the wake of the life-size cross.

Watching all these Christians in the procession on the *Via Crucis* makes me think of a phrase from the days of Vatican II: a "Church of sinners." We, the "Church of saints" cheered the Messiah on Palm Sunday. Today we, the "Church of sinners," are the guilty mob on Calvary.

The palm branches have an interesting role in all of this. The saints on earth carry them in the crowd on Palm Sunday as symbols of our belief in Jesus as the Messiah. Some saints carry them in the Good Friday procession as a reminder of our weakness and unfaithfulness. But the palm branches don't disappear with the burial of Jesus. No, they show up one last time in every saint's story. In the Book of Revelation, St. John tells us

> *After that I saw that there was a huge number, impossible*
> *for anyone to count, of people from every nation, race, tribe*
> *and language; they were standing in front of the throne and*
> *in front of the Lamb, dressed in white robes and holding*
> *palms in their hands. They shouted in a loud voice, "Salva-*
> *tion to our God, who sits on the throne, and to the Lamb!"*

In the victory celebration in heaven, all the saints will be carrying palms. The branches will be the sign of our sharing in Christ's final triumph over sin, over our unfaithfulness and over death itself.

The procession has left the church now. A few dozen people have stayed behind to go to confession. I walk over and sit on a hard wooden chair in the little open alcove that will be my confessional. The first penitent, a sun-dried old man, shuffles toward me. A well-worn palm branch is clutched in his gnarled brown hand. Will he bring it with him once again, I wonder, when he comes to celebrate on Easter Sunday?

The Support Group

St. Julien le Pauvre, Paris

With its rough stone walls and low Romanesque lines, it looks like a village church that has lost its way and stumbled, bewildered, into one of the noisiest neighborhoods of Paris. Just across the river from the great Gothic towers of Notre Dame, I step through a modest doorway into the dimly lit Church of St. Julien le Pauvre.

It still keeps the humble simplicity it had when it served as a shrine for medieval pilgrims on their way to Compostela. In recent years, its charming, intimate interior has made the church a popular spot for chamber music concerts.

I find a seat in the second row—my reward for coming early. Glancing over the evening's printed program, I recognize the titles of several familiar pieces by Mozart, Vivaldi and Handel. There is still plenty of time to gaze around and take in the scene.

The simple round arches, dark vaults, and small windows give me the sense of closeness that I've felt in little parish churches in farming towns. Recently, St. Julien was given to the Greek Orthodox Church for their regular worship space, and now a colorful *iconostasis*—a wooden partition decorated with hand-painted icons—is built across the front of the apse and hung with flickering votive candles. This adds a touch of life and color to the otherwise somber beauty of the place. In the narrow, brightly lit area between this altar screen and the front row of the audience, eight empty chairs face outward and wait self-consciously for the members of the string ensemble to make their appearance.

My imagination fills the church with pilgrims assembling to start out on a pilgrimage to Compostela early tomorrow morning. I can almost hear the church's bell ring out as it did for centuries to call the students to their classes at the nearby Sorbonne.

From the rear of the church, a ripple of applause grows to a wave as the musicians, clad in traditional black-and-white formal dress, walk briskly down the left aisle and take their seats in the sanctuary. The first violinist will also act as conductor of the group. There is a final muted tune-up, then a couple of seconds of pregnant silence. Finally the instruments burst into a robust rendition of Mozart's *Eine Kleine Nachtmusik.*

"Bomp, ba-bomp, ba-bomp ba-bomp ba-BOMP!" The young man playing the bass violin is obviously enjoying himself, his expressive face letting everyone know that this is one of his favorite pieces. A young woman with her black hair pulled back in a severe bun, on the other hand, plays her viola precisely; her only goal seems to be technical perfection. The woman to her right, with short brown hair, looks as though she loves playing, but seems a little bit tired. I wonder if she's a mother who has had to hire a baby-sitter for the evening, and has left the supper dishes in the sink. The unkempt first violinist has a lot of the showman about him and is deliberately swinging the far end of his violin in expansive circles. I look once again at the bass player. For the last few moments he has not been playing, but simply standing with his eyes closed, nodding his approval of the violin passage and smiling at the little surprises that Mozart slips in now and then.

The second movement already, the Andante: "Da, da, DAH . . . dee DAH-da DAH-da DAH-da-DAH!" The first violinist is now drawing acrobatic figure eights for us with the scroll-end of his instrument while never missing a note.

I seldom get to music recitals when I'm home in the monastery, but have to content myself with recordings of the great artists and orchestras on tapes or on some FM station. There really is something special about a live performance. First, of course, there is the sense of human contact as you get to know the lively bass player, the young mother with the viola, and the egomaniac on first violin. But even more gratifying than "getting to know" the musicians, is the presence of something you never hear on a compact disc recording at home: imperfections!

These performers in front of me are professionals, and they're good. Every now and then, however, maybe just once in a whole concert, somebody will leave a trail of muddy notes where there should have been sparkling diamonds. *Hrumph!* complains the little critic inside of me, *On my recording at home, Bruno Walter and the Columbia Symphony Orchestra do a much better job on that passage!*

Oh! Here's the third movement, the Allegretto: "Da-DUMP-dum, dah DAH, da DUMP dump, dah DA-da DA-da Da-da . . ." The bass violinist sticks the tip of his tongue out of the corner of his mouth as he concentrates on moving his fingers nimbly through a particularly delicious bass run. Suddenly he breaks into a broad smile as if he's enjoying a personal joke.

As I watch and listen, it dawns on me that what I hear on a digital compact disc is probably a thoroughly sanitized performance. There are no friendly background noises of squeaking chairs and stifled coughs. All the imperfections have been removed electronically, all the poor passages redone, and every blemish cosmetically removed by clever audio engineers. The notes have been reduced to a series of zeroes and ones in a computer and then put back together on the disk.

No fancy audio tricks here in St. Julien tonight, though! These musicians are real people who have families and friends. They eat lunch, smoke cigarettes, ride the métro, and discuss politics like everybody else. Each of them contributes his or her talent to the group, and together they are making the stone vaults ring with the heavenly harmonies of Mozart. They play quite well together, no doubt about it. Still, this is a group of human beings, so they're not perfect.

None of them seems preoccupied with being perfect, either—with the possible exception of the woman with the black hair. I study her stern face for a moment and start to feel vaguely uneasy. Suddenly I realize why I don't like that forbidding but familiar expression: It's *my* face, my "work" face. Whenever I do a job, my unconscious goal is always to do it perfectly. It is, needless to say, a bit of a strain on coworkers and brother monks, and on me, too. During this year away, I'm getting a chance to step back from my perfectionism and look at it from the outside, the way I'm looking at this violist. And I don't like what I see . . .

The fourth and last movement of *Eine Kleine*, the Allegro. They're really moving this one along: "DRRRIN-din, din-din, DUNT-dunt-Dun!" The young bassist is throwing himself body and soul into the marvelous off-beats of the bass line, so "into" the music that he's playing it from the inside out. He's so uplifted and enthralled by the beauty of what the group is creating up there that he has left any concerns about perfection far, far behind . . .

Beauty and harmony are things we can all achieve in our lives, but perfection is not—that's reserved for God alone. Imperfect musicians who still make such beautiful music together remind me that I don't need to be a perfect saint, a perfect monk, or a perfect anything else. I just need to concentrate on making music with my fellow saints in the monastery and in school, music that isn't perfect—only beautiful.

In a flash of insight I see the truth about myself: I am a recovering perfectionist! I immediately promise myself to attend these concerts faithfully, hoping vaguely that these musicians will be a support group. As the audience breaks into heartfelt applause, the musicians stand and acknowledge our enthusiasm. I'm already looking forward to our next meeting.

Rue du Grenier sur l'Eau   Paris

Part Two
Saints on My Street

Via Dei Neri - Florence

God's Country

Florence, Italy

My head is full of gondolas and canals, arched bridges and flocks of pigeons. I've spent the last few days living with my brother Benedictines at the island abbey of San Giorgio in the middle of the bay of Venice. But now I'm on a train heading south to Tuscany. I changed trains a few minutes ago in Florence and am taking a half-hour ride out to the ancient monastery of Benedictine nuns in Pontassieve, where I'll be staying for the next four days.

I glance out of the window and . . . wait a minute! I've never been anywhere near this part of Italy before, so why do I have the distinct feeling that I know this place? Those odd cypresses that look like great green feathers are familiar, for example. So is the little river that winds among castle-topped hills until it's lost in the blue-gray haze of the distance. Then I realize what's going on: I've been looking at these scenes my whole life in the backgrounds of famous paintings! These great Florentine artists are so familiar that we call them by their first names—Michelangelo, Rafael, Leonardo. Their paintings are so much a part of our religious imagery that we take it for granted that Mary visited Elizabeth in an Italian villa with cypress trees in the background and that both women were dressed as Renaissance ladies. I look out the window again half expecting to see the Angel Gabriel suddenly appear on that marble terrace over there unrolling a long white banner in front of a young Virgin: "*Ave, gratia plena!*" On the road in the distance I search for the exotic procession of camels carrying the Three Kings and their gifts to a chubby Florentine *bambino* lying in the courtyard of that big farmhouse near the tracks.

The little train rattles along hillsides that are covered with vineyards and topped with towers, and follows the banks of the Arno past fallow fields, exhausted little garden plots, and genteelly decaying farm houses.

The artists showed deep theological insight when they placed the great events of salvation in familiar landscapes close to home. People looking at the paintings would have had the sense that these great mysteries had happened right in their own territory. When an artist paints an Annunciation scene, he makes sure to let us glimpse through an open window that this is happening right here in the town where he is painting. He wants us to recognize the familiar hills, the little bridge and the city walls. When the shepherds come to visit the manger, the artist places the stable in his native Italy, in a spot just outside of Florence. Jesus, the painter is telling us, is born in our own midst. When Jesus preaches his sermon on the Mount, he stands on a hill with the familiar bends of the Arno river in the background, speaking to people who look like typical townspeople of Tuscany.

These artists help us to do what St. Benedict in his Holy Rule asks his monks to do: "always be mindful of the presence of God." This mindfulness of God's constant, continuing presence in our lives is sometimes called the "fear of God." It doesn't mean cringing terror, but simply a clear awareness of this God who is present everywhere.

Dozens of chattering high-schoolers pile onto the train, enlivening the dreary grown-up atmosphere with their rowdy laughing and loud kidding . . .

And then, I realize: the message of the great Italian masterpieces has gotten completely turned around. Ironically, for us citizens of the New World, the pictures do just the opposite of what their makers intended. They now encourage not the constant mindfulness of God's presence, but rather what St. Benedict calls *oblivio*, forgetfulness.

These paintings assure us that God's great deeds were done in some place far, far away. Bethlehem, where God became flesh, is an unreal land of feather-shaped trees and castle-topped hills! The Christ child grew up in an idealized village in Tuscany—certainly nowhere around where I live. If the Way of the Cross winds through a quaint Italian town with a wall around it, then Jesus isn't as likely to show up in my town, in my neighborhood.

Some of us would prefer to forget that Jesus is present everywhere with his power and love, because that Jesus also has a way of making demands on us. We'd prefer God to be elsewhere, at some safe distance. If we keep Jesus slightly alien, we won't see him at our supper table or in our workplace. We won't have to hear his voice challenging us.

Across the aisle, a young mother holds her baby on her lap. At her feet is a diaper bag, and on the bench beside her is the baby's half-eaten cracker.

What would people think of a picture of Mary playing with Jesus not on an Italian hillside (which is somehow quite acceptable) but on the seat of a passenger train? Somehow it doesn't fit: Mary and Jesus don't have anything to do with the real mothers and babies of today. God's love doesn't walk among us the way it did for Rafael and Michelangelo.

The saint is one who cultivates the sense that God is present in every place. The saint won't let God be confined to churches, convents, and Vatican City—or to some Renaissance landscape in Tuscany. The saint won't let God's great works be limited to "elsewhere." The saint accepts that Jesus healed lepers in Judea and in fifteenth-century Tuscany but can see him at work also in our own hospitals and sickrooms. The saint can pray with great devotion in front of a painting of a Christ who is suffering and dying in the streets of some Italian village, but can also recognize him dying with heroin in his veins in our own town. For the saint, it is decidedly *not somewhere else* that God works wonders.

Pontassieve. I shove myself and my suitcase down the aisle and squeeze through the knot of friendly teenagers smoking in the vestibule. They watch me climb awkwardly down the steep train steps. I land with a jolt on the platform in front of a handsome young man with long black hair who is waiting for the next train. I get a funny feeling as I look at him. Hmm . . . where have I seen that face before?

The Man Who Led Two Lives
Padua, Italy

I'm on a walking tour of Padua, following the free map provided by the Tourist Office. I started at the railroad station (the first stop on the map) and have followed the red line painted on the sidewalk. It has already led past ancient Roman walls, down busy streets and across wide piazzas, passing the great brown basilica of *Il Santo*, St. Anthony of Padua, wonder-worker and finder of lost articles, and has started to circle back after reaching the immense church of Santa Giustina, the patron saint of the city.

My own patron saint, Albert the Great, was a Dominican scholar. His tremendous breadth of knowledge in physical sciences, philosophy, and theology earned him the title of *Doctor Universalis*, "Universal Doctor." I have walked in his footsteps a couple of times already in my European travels. In Paris, I strolled down the quiet street named after him: *rue du Maître Albert*, "Master Albert Street," on the Left Bank. It was near there that he studied and taught from 1241 to 1248. In Cologne, I stayed for a few days with the Dominican Friars at Sankt Andreas Kirche, the lovely Romanesque church where Albert's body lies in a plain stone sarcophagus in the crypt. On today's day-trip from Venice, I hope to meet up with the great Doctor of the Church once again, this time at the University of Padua.

The University is a large blue "56" printed over a busy shopping street in the center of my map. I follow the red line toward the spot, watching for my patron's footprints . . .

The official date of the founding of the great school is 1222. The very next summer, Jordan of Saxony, the successor of St. Dominic as master general of the Dominicans, comes to Padua in hopes of attracting candidates to the new Order of Preachers. Among his ten recruits, he writes, are "two sons of two great German lords, one . . . has resigned rich benefices and is truly noble in mind and body." Tradition has it that the second young man is the future *Albertus Magnus*, St. Albert the Great.

For its first 300 years, the University didn't even have its own buildings, so I'm not likely to find any places where young Albert actually studied. What I do find this afternoon are plenty of worn-out four-story buildings with modern shops on the street level. I cross avenues filled with noisy noonday traffic and stroll along crowded sidewalks. The red line takes me past computer stores, leather boutiques, trattorias, florists, and booksellers to the spot shown on my map. But I don't see any university. There is, however, a marker that brags that Professor Galileo Galilei perfected the telescope while teaching here between 1592 and 1608.

I remember being fascinated as a college student by the life of a philosopher who taught in the University of Padua at about the same time as Galileo. He had the unforgettable name of Professor Pietro Pomponazzi. What was even more impressive than his name was his double life. A devout, practicing Catholic, he would go to church and worship God, then walk to the university and teach his students that the truths of philosophy and logic completely contradict those of faith. He taught that according to philosophy the soul cannot be immortal, but that according to theology it is. He saw no problem in holding both teachings as true.

My philosophical musings are rudely interrupted by the screech of brakes and the ill-tempered blast of a horn. I've just stepped off the curb and am blinking stupidly at the red Ferrari that has almost hit me. The driver screams at me in loud Italian and roars off flourishing some quaint hand gesture that undoubtedly dates back to the days of the obscene Emperor Caligula.

Professor Pomponazzi led two separate lives. First, he was a loyal Catholic, holding to the beliefs and practices of the Church. Second, he was a philosopher, following the strict demands of reason and the laws of evidence, the conclusions of which were often at odds with the teachings of his faith. He somehow managed to hold that both contradictory sets of beliefs were true—he simply kept them entirely separated from one another in his mind.

It's interesting that the Oration of the mass for the feast of Albert the Great says that the saint was known for his "talent of combining human wisdom and divine faith." Unlike Pomponazzi, Albert did not lead two lives. He saw everything he did, whether in biology, chemistry, or philosophy, as somehow infused with the holy, with the presence of God.

Finding no trace of anything that looks like a school building, I take it on faith that I'm standing right in the middle of the famous university where Albert studied and Pietro Pomponazzi taught. I decide to keep following the faithful red line back to the railroad station.

In a slightly different way from my professor friend, many modern Christians see themselves as leading two lives. First, there is the life that has to do with God, angels, heaven, and hell. This is called "religion." At most, it demands an hour on Sunday, the avoidance of gross sins, and intellectual agreement with a set of doctrines. Second, and more important, there are the everyday concerns of earning a living, making the car payments, changing diapers, and keeping the house in order. This is called "real life." Since many Christians can see little or no connection between their religious beliefs and the practicalities of their "real" life, they lead two distinct lives that at times are even opposed to each other.

In fact, though, as St. Albert knew, it is in just such so-called "secular" things that we are most likely to meet God. A young mother's spirituality revolves around feeding and caring for her child. A middle-aged man who is considering changing careers suddenly learns what it means to trust in God's goodness. His insecure job situation certainly involves weighing such factors as salary and job satisfaction, but it is also the place where he is going to meet—right now—the God who loves him and watches over him.

Every Christian is called to experience God's unconditional love working itself out in everyday events. For the young mother, for the fellow afraid of changing careers, for all of us, it's never a question of "prayer life" versus "real life." Saints don't lead two lives, but one. Our everyday experiences challenge us to grow in trust or to risk loving someone or to be compassionate. We can accept these opportunities or not, but we can't say that they have nothing to do with our spiritual life.

The train station looms up ahead. The red line has brought me back to my starting point after a pleasant day in the company of an unlikely group: Saint Anthony and his lost articles, Galileo and his telescope, Albert the Great and his books, and Pietro Pomponazzi, the man who led two lives.

God Slips In

Brussels, Belgium

The *musée national de l'art ancien,* the national art museum in Brussels, is filled, as I expected, with a spectacular collection of Flemish and Dutch paintings. I wander past masterpieces by Frans Hals, Rembrandt, and Van Dyck: portraits of well-fed merchants wearing wide lace collars and self-satisfied smiles. I gape at the weird prophetic fantasies of Hieronymus Bosch, whose strange goblin creatures ride on the backs of pterodactyls and toss bombs onto the bizarre blue landscape far below.

I'm here in search of my favorite painting, by Peter Bruegel the Elder. I come at last into a room full of paintings by the two Bruegels, father and son, and easily recognize the charming rural scenes and the brown, gray, and russet earth tones of the elder Bruegel. I pause in front of his *The Slaughter of the Holy Innocents.*

Bruegel has set the biblical story in his own country and his own century: the occupying troops are not Roman legionnaires but Spanish soldiers. I watch in fascinated horror as men in silver breastplates and helmets raid a country village in Bruegel's native Flanders. Under the approving eye of their commander, they are stabbing little babies as terrified mothers scream in horror and try in vain to protect their children. The painter's own pain and sorrow give the scene more realism and emotional impact than any other depiction of this story I've ever seen.

Since this is in fact the companion piece to my favorite painting, I scan the other walls expectantly . . . Soon I begin to wonder if the picture I came to see may be out on loan or temporarily removed for restoration. With fingers crossed I move on into the next room, where there are more Bruegels. Turning to my left, I break into a relieved smile as I recognize my old familiar friend: *The Numbering at Bethlehem.*

The canvas, about six feet long and three-and-a-half feet high, depicts a snowy winter scene in a busy little sixteenth-century Flemish village. The painting is buzzing with the activities of daily life: chickens are scratching the snow for food, children are playing on the ice and throwing snowballs, a butcher is slaughtering a pig in front of his shop, men are warming themselves around an outdoor fire, and a young man is courting a maid as they skate on the river. Off to the left, people cluster patiently in the cold as an official at an open window writes their names in a fat book.

This is the painter's interpretation of the scene in Bethlehem as Jews "from the House of David" came to register for the census decreed by Caesar Augustus. Bruegel and his countrymen in sixteenth-century Brabant could identify with the Jews of Jesus' time. The Netherlands was suffering under the oppressive rule of the King of Spain in the same way that Judea had once shivered in the ominous shadow of the Emperor of Rome, who had ordered the census.

Searching carefully among the tiny, busy figures near the center of the picture, I pick out a brown-robed man. The large saw he is carrying over his shoulder shows that he is a carpenter. He's leading a little gray donkey on which is seated a young woman bundled in a blue blanket. I can feel the sharp cold on my cheeks and hear the delighted shrieks of the children and the squeal of the unfortunate pig. The smell of wood smoke sours the air. As the couple and their donkey trudge wearily past me in the snow, I notice that the young woman, who is obviously pregnant, looks drawn and tired. No one in the village is paying the least attention to them. The children are absorbed in their play, the butchers and the merchants are going about their business, and the grim-faced officials are taking their census. The carpenter turns the donkey toward the crowded inn. The sad sun hangs like a frozen orange in the black skeleton of a tree.

Two other visitors to the museum come and stand next to me for a moment and glance at the painting. I ask myself, "Do they see Joseph and Mary? What if they don't know enough to look for the man with the saw and the girl on the donkey?" I'm bursting to poke one of them and whisper, "Psst! Do you see them? They're right there, in the middle, next to the man at the big wine barrel!" But I hold myself back, and in a few seconds the visitors move on.

Peter Bruegel's painting reminds us that Christmas is a very subtle feast—a celebration of God's bashful, self-giving love and infinite humility. The dull, understated colors in the painting convey this subtlety so perfectly that tourists in the museum look right at the picture without seeing what it is really about. It is, of course, about love, Love that became a human being and dwelt among us. But love comes quietly, even mysteriously sometimes. The scene of the poor Flemish village occupied by foreign troops reminds us that God, like love itself, is somehow linked with the mystery of human suffering and the shadowy side of life. We can almost hear the oppressed villagers in the painting complaining, at the very moment that the couple with the donkey walk past them, "Where is God? Why is God so far away and unconcerned about our lives?"

This is why the holiday season always brings that awful letdown, that almost inevitable sense of disappointment. It is not simply that reality can never live up to our idealized childhood memories or the romanticized scenes of Christmas we see on television. A more fundamental reason lies in the mystery of Christmas itself: after all of the "hype" from the Old Testament prophets about the future Prince of Peace, after all of the Advent preparation for the coming of the "Desire of Nations," Salvation finally arrives and what do we see? Just a tired couple with a baby. God has come to save us, sure, but as nothing more than an infant, a bundle of possibility, powerless and mute, vulnerable and unrecognizable. This is the built-in disappointment of Christmas. But this is also its greatness.

It is only in coming as a baby that God can assure the powerless that salvation doesn't lie in might and mastery. It is only by being born in a stable that God can persuade the poor that salvation doesn't lie in wealth and economic security. It is only by being born unnoticed in the obscurity of a small town that the King of Kings can convince the unloved that our salvation doesn't lie in fame or popularity. Emmanuel, God-with-us, comes as Mystery to be seen only with the eyes of faith. God comes as a surprise, in a shocking reversal of this world's wisdom.

Most of us don't recognize Jesus when he appears in our lives. It might not look like Christmas when Emmanuel walks into a hospital room and uses my voice to give a cheering word to a depressed patient, but how else is the Messiah to arrive "with healing in his wings"? It might not look like Christmas when a busy parent takes the time to sit down and go over a third-grader's homework with her, but how else is Wisdom from on High to visit us? It might not look like Christmas when someone refuses to join in an office joke that degrades women or some racial minority, but how else is the Prince of Peace or the Sun of Justice to dawn in our hearts?

Emmanuel, God-with-us, enters the cold, busy villages of our lives all the time, often unfelt and unrecognized, the way the carpenter and his wife slip into this Flemish hamlet in the snow.

A man in a blue suit walks into the center of the room and announces in a commanding voice that the museum is closing in a few minutes and everyone has to leave. I take one final look at my favorite painting: a gray afternoon in a rundown village. No, it doesn't look a bit like Christmas.

Benedictine Abbey Church (18th C) Tihany Hungary

Love, the Guest
Gödöllő, Hungary

It's Christmas Eve, and for the first time in over thirty years, I'm not celebrating it in the monastery. Instead I'm holding the hand of Szófi, a bright, blonde five-year-old who is skipping and jumping on her way back from church after the traditional Christmas Pageant. Her aunt, a friend of mine, is holding her other hand as we hurry through the cold Hungarian afternoon in Gödöllő, a small town twenty miles north of Budapest.

The parish church is actually the chapel of the famous Grassalkovich chateau, a great house that is being slowly restored after many years of abandonment and neglect. Built in 1744, the mansion was given as a coronation present to the Emperor Franz Joseph I in 1867, who made it his family's summer residence. The baroque chapel of this "royal summer palace" was the setting for our afternoon's drama, with children playing all the roles. There was Mary, of course, and Joseph, the baby, and the shepherds. I think that St. Francis of Assisi got involved, too, along with a couple of wicked robbers who, if I'm guessing correctly, were converted through the efforts of the Saint.

The scheduling of the children's Christmas program for the afternoon of December 24 is carefully calculated. It's a convenient way to get the children out of the house so that "Baby Jesus and the angels" can come and put up the Christmas tree in the living room and set out the holiday presents. This year it is also a good way to arrange a few hours of quiet time for Szófi's mother who is due to give birth to her second child any time now.

On the walk home in the chilly, darkening afternoon we start to look into the windows of the austere Communist-era apartment buildings. Szófi spots the first Christmas tree, its colored electric lights sparkling gaily through the curtains of someone's second floor apartment. She shouts excitedly and lets go of my hand to point at the window. I don't really need her aunt's translation: "She says that Jesus and the angels have visited that house over there." Soon we spot another lighted tree, and then another. "She says Baby Jesus has been all over Gödöllő this afternoon." And because of his visit these buildings seem brighter and happier places. Jumping with excitement, Szófi can't wait to get back to her grandparents' apartment to see.

It's not too far now, and Szófi is pulling us along faster and faster. We keep spotting more Christmas trees through people's windows, more signs of Baby Jesus' presence.

At last we're in the hallway of the apartment building, and the delicious smells of Christmas cooking float down the stairs. When Grandpa opens the door for us, I don't understand his words, but I can guess from the tone of his voice and the shake of his head that Szófi's mom still hasn't had the baby. A question from Szófi draws a big smile from him. I recognize the Hungarian word "Egen!"—"Yes!" And the name "Jesus." "Yes," he must be telling her, "Baby Jesus has been here and he's put the tree in the living room!" My five-year-old friend, bursting with curiosity, squirms impatiently as Grandpa finishes unbuttoning her coat. Finally free of his clutches, she walks briskly down the hall, leading Grandma, Grandpa, Aunt Babi, and me in an impromptu procession. I try to catch up to her before she turns the corner into the little living room—I want to watch the expression on her face when she sees that Baby Jesus has really come, just as he promised.

I am not disappointed. Her eyes fill with wonder at the realization that Baby Jesus has actually come right into her grandparents' apartment this afternoon and made it a special, holy place.

I start to hum to myself the words of an Advent carol:

> Make your house fair as you are able,
> Trim the hearth and set the table,
> People look East, and sing to today,
> Love, the guest, is on the way.

Szófi's delight makes me stop and ask myself, *What would it be like if we really took seriously the idea that Jesus was coming to our house as a guest? Would we have to scramble to make ourselves and our homes presentable?* Would some favorite television programs have to be skipped to avoid embarrassing the Guest? Would there be more patience and fewer sarcastic remarks during family conversations?

Suddenly it dawns on me: "You know, *she's right!*" When she peeks into the living room Szófi sees the deeper truth that we grownups usually miss: the Christmas tree and the presents so lovingly arranged by her grandparents really *are* the handiwork of Jesus! This is no fairy tale, but a basic belief of our faith: love and selfless giving are the sign and the actual presence of Christ in our midst. Christ is with us "wherever two or three are gathered" in his name. Christ is among us in the person of the poor, the oppressed, the child, the sick. Christ is present wherever there is self-giving love, kindness, or gentleness. The saint can spot these presences everywhere and be cheered by them the way Szófi is when she sees Christmas trees glowing in people's windows.

Although this Christmas Eve isn't as solemn or silent as it would be in the monastery, it's teaching me to see the world once again with the eyes of a saint, the way little Szófi does. I glance at her grandparents and her aunt. They are still waiting, preoccupied with joyful hope as they wait for Marta to give birth. This Christmas, they can hardly wait to welcome God's grace and joy into their hearts and into their home—in the form of a helpless newborn baby.

> *People look East, and sing to today,*
> *Love, the guest, is on the way.*

Florence 1450

The Sacred Bath

Poitiers, France

To get to the city of Poitiers from the train station, I walk up a long, winding staircase that climbs the cliff behind which the town is presumably hiding. Out of breath at the top of the stairs, I find myself gaping up at the marvelous twelfth-century church of Saint Hilaire le Grand. It's named after St. Hilary, bishop of Poitiers in the mid-300s, who wrote with deep insight about the mystery of the Holy Trinity and who successfully fended off the Arians by showing that Jesus was truly God as well as truly human.

A fifteen-minute walk through some thoroughly nondescript old streets brings me across town to a tiny but very venerable building that lies partially buried in the center of a busy traffic circle. This is the baptistery of St. John, the oldest Christian structure in all of France, dating from about A.D. 290.

During my walk, I can't help thinking of a day in September of 1356 when the good citizens lined the tops of these town walls to watch the Battle of Poitiers. The vastly outnumbered English army crushed the French forces and headed for the coast, dragging with them as their prisoner the French king, who was to fetch a hefty ransom.

I now find myself standing in the plaza in front of the city's jewel, the church of Notre-Dame-la-Grande. Across the facade of this twelfth-century church, fourteen carved saints stand solemnly in their niches, forever frozen in neat rows on either side of the central window. The paint which once enlivened the stone figures with bright colors has long since worn off, and the twelve apostles' features have weathered into a certain gray sameness that gives the whole group a pleasant unity.

Beneath this collection of saints is a strip of smaller carvings of bible stories. Toward its right-hand end I can make out scenes from the life of the Virgin Mary after whom the church is named. One of these catches my eye. What is she doing? Could it be? Yes! Here, in full view of staid, historic Poitiers, surrounded by the twelve apostles and two other saints, Mary of Nazareth is giving her baby a bath!

St. Hilary, bishop of Poitiers, had doggedly defended the doctrine that Jesus was God, yet here the Divine Word stands hidden to his little waist in a big bathtub with his mother holding him up by the arms. Actually the image of God getting shampoo in his eyes doesn't shock me. After all, we Christians meditate daily on far worse things than that happening to Jesus. No, what unsettles me is the idea of Mary getting splashed.

I've visited many of the great museums of the Western world, and I've thumbed through books of Christian art for decades, so I think I know how this is supposed to work. Mary is to be found praying in her room, or kneeling in awed adoration beside the manger. She weeps in silent dignity at the foot of the cross or sits in marble coldness holding her dead son on her lap. She rides on the clouds of heaven or is crowned by Christ in glory. At her most undignified, she's sometimes caught riding a donkey. But I've never seen a picture of Mary getting the washcloth thrown in her face or grabbing for the bottle of baby oil just as the Christ child is about to toss it into the tub.

As I watch, Mary lets go of one of the divine wrists to push a few stray hairs back under her veil, and the baby takes quick advantage to reach down with his fat little hand and slap at the water. His mother, naturally, gets splashed full in the face— a treatment familiar to millions of mothers before and since. With a look of startled surprise, she stares down at her soaked dress. Clucking her tongue in mild exasperation she tries to grab the slippery arm before more damage is done. I notice for the first time how much the squirming little boy looks like his mother, especially around the mouth and eyes. The futile attempts to capture the offending arm quickly become a playful contest between mother and baby, and their laughter carries across the church plaza. Delighted with the new game, he slaps a fistful of bath water up at the dignified St. Peter who is standing nearby holding two big keys. By this time all the saints in their colorful robes are looking down at the scene and laughing. Peter is roaring with delight as he dries off the keys to the kingdom.

Suddenly the facade is gray, lifeless stone again. What have I seen? It must have been some devilish deception. Surely Mary, whom the litany calls "Tower of Ivory," and "Ark of the Covenant," Mary, the Queen of Heaven, never put on an apron, rolled back those flowing white sleeves, and gave her baby a bath!

This simple little scene in Poitiers is a powerful reminder to all would-be saints. The bath is sacred because God is present there. And a God who can fit into a baby's bathtub can surely fit into my workplace or my kitchen or the shopping mall. Most of us become saints by meeting God faithfully in just such ordinary places, and by relating with God through our coworkers, spouses, and friends.

The Church has canonized hosts of nuns and monks for being exemplary, humble religious. Maybe one day soon we'll start decorating our parish churches with statues of single layfolks, of husbands and wives, of moms and dads, honoring these saints for being faithful friends, helpful neighbors, loving spouses, or dedicated parents.

My train leaves in half an hour, and it's a long walk back to the station. Reluctantly I turn and head across the plaza. Just before rounding the corner I sneak a last quick glance over my shoulder. There are the apostles, standing stony and stiff. There is the Blessed Mother in the lowest row, off to the right, still giving the Son of God his bath. But I swear her dress looks wet.

Castle of
Vajdahunyad
in Budapest

Part Three
Holy Combat

Keeping Watch

Eger, Hungary

A blistering August sun makes the climb seem steeper than it really is. As my three Hungarian hosts and I trudge up a dusty approach road to the ruins at the top of this hill in northeastern Hungary, I recall the story of the heroes of the siege of Eger. Every Hungarian schoolchild knows it . . .

During the summer of 1552, two Turkish armies had captured thirty Hungarian strongholds with little trouble, and figured to take the fortress of Eger just as easily. As we reach the entrance gate at the top, it's clear why the Turks expected to make short work of it. Eger is in a poor strategic position: hills rise above its eastern and northern sides, offering attackers perfect placements for short-range guns and a view of everything going on inside the walls below. And yet, the Hungarian commander, István Dobo, and his two thousand brave men and women held off forty thousand Turks on this spot for thirty-nine gruesome days, persevering until the frustrated attackers simply gave up and went home in disgrace. The heroic deeds of the defenders have been retold ever since in song, story, and poem.

We pass through the gate and onto a dusty field surrounded by low stone walls and a few reconstructed buildings. I can feel that this is indeed a sacred site, a place baptized in blood.

During that famous siege in the summer of 1552, the sandstone walls were pounded into rubble by enemy cannons, but enough of the ruins remain to give my imagination plenty to play with. We stand on the north wall looking across a small ravine at the facing hill that once swarmed with turbaned Turkish soldiers. It's as if the siege guns have just stopped their constant booming, and there is an eerie quiet before the next attack . . .

Here they come! Wave upon wave of *janissaries, saabs, delis,* and *djebedjis,* screaming "*Allah akbar*" as they storm the walls, trying to plant their red pennants on the ramparts. Clouds of choking black smoke belch from cannons and rifles. The ingenious exploding devices of Gergeley Bornemissza start belching fire and death, sowing panic in the ranks of the Turks.

The desperate Hungarian defenders have already beaten off several frenzied assaults, and Turkish corpses are beginning to pile up at the foot of Eger's ramparts. So the wily Turkish commander has added another tactic: his men are digging a tunnel under the walls, planning to come up inside the stronghold and catch the Hungarians by surprise. But here in the fort, commander Dobo, being no stranger to such tricks himself, suspects that the Turks are burrowing beneath the walls of Eger. And he has a solution: all the way around the inside of the wall, at set intervals, he puts simple peasant bowls filled with water to act as detectors. Each time a sentry comes to one of these bowls he will stop and watch the surface of the water for telltale ripples . . .

We walk up a flight of stone steps and through the remains of a small building. The stables must have been over here . . .

A few days later a breathless guard races up to his commander, "Sir! Come quickly! The bowl in the stable! The water's moving!" They crowd into the empty stall and lean over the peasant bowl to watch excitedly. Sure enough, there in the torch light, tiny ripples, too small to notice without staring, are making ominous rings in the water. Those little waves tell of a deadly scheme unfolding under their very feet. Deep beneath the wall of the fortress, the Turks are busy tunneling. The hapless diggers, planning a surprise attack, will now get a deadly shock themselves when they finally break through.

The early Church was fond of the image of Christian life as "holy combat" fought on the battlefield of the human heart. This image warns us that although we are already saved through the mystery of Jesus' life, death, and resurrection, we still need to struggle daily against the enemies who attack us. Our own self-centeredness, our "spoiled child," our "false self": there is a real wisdom in watching out for these and other enemies that can keep us from being who we're called to be.

I've seen more than one person burst out in a fit of childish anger or cruel selfishness and then look around, appalled at the wreckage they've just caused, and ask themselves, *Where did* that *come from?* I can think of a few times when I've been caught completely off guard by some totally unexpected outburst of my own pettiness or plain nastiness.

If I don't want to be taken by surprise by my emotions and inner drives, I can learn a lesson from the heroes of Eger whose sentries kept a careful eye on those bowls of water placed on the ground. I have my own bowls that bear watching, signals that reveal something of my inner life to me. Sometimes they are as small as passing feelings or brief interchanges with others.

Of course I may be justified in being a little upset at finding that someone's put an empty cereal box back in the cupboard, but this time the petty annoyance triggers a burst of furious anger. Suddenly an image flashes in front of me: A bowl of water is sitting on the dirt floor of a fortress, and on the surface of the water are tiny disturbances. Like those ripples that were barely visible but gave a valuable warning about what was happening underneath the fortress of Eger, my outburst is a very useful tip-off: I need to ask myself what is really bothering me—something deeper, at work beneath the surface of my life. Maybe an incident that happened yesterday in a meeting or some bad news about a close friend last night upset me more than I realized. My flare-up becomes both a useful warning and a clear challenge to unearth the real but hidden issue and deal with it somehow.

The Hungarian sentry had been taught the meaning of the ripples on the water and was on the watch for them. We, too, have our own bowls of water, and like that sentry, we can make use of them. They can alert us if, beneath the calm surface of our lives, there is an unseen problem that demands attention. They can make us aware of some unpleasant truth about ourselves that we've been reluctant to face.

"Well, are you ready to go? We're all getting hot and tired!" My friend's words bring me out of my musing with a jolt.

The heat is now pouring up from the dust in heavy sheets. My three Hungarian hosts and I agree that it's time to call it quits. Hot and exhausted, we trudge back down the long road the way we came, like the tired Turks of 1552.

Staying Prepared

Fulda, Germany

The snow outside is streaming past the train window in those tiny flakes that promise a lot more to come. Central Germany is covered with a white blanket three inches deep. The table in front of me is covered with my things: paperback book, breviary, notebook, travel guides, and a small bag of pretzels. Buried under the debris is a single sheet of paper provided by the German railroad company, listing the time of arrival for each town, as well as the main connecting trains that can be met at each of the stations on our route. We've just pulled in for a three-minute stop at Fulda.

I peer out the window into the cottony whiteness and can't see much of anything. But my mind's eye goes to work with no trouble—the name Fulda evokes all sorts of history for a Benedictine . . .

I imagine I can see the cathedral built originally as the Benedictine Abbey church in the early 1700s. Then there is the monastery itself, which became famous when St. Boniface, the Apostle of Germany, lived here as a monk for ten years before his martyrdom in 754. In the next century the abbey would grow to more than 400 monks, and would boast a renowned *scriptorium* and an influential monastery school. For three hundred years, it was the most important imperial abbey in Germany, producing masterpieces in manuscript illumination and murals, in gold work and sculpture.

I stop staring out at the snow, and my eye wanders down to the table in front of me. I notice the corner of the train schedule peeking out from under my pencil case. I pull it out and start to read it in an absentminded way. *Let's see . . . Here we are, Fulda—Right on time. There are even a couple of connecting trains you can catch at Fulda. Hmm! An express train for Munich comes in five minutes, and arrives in Munich at 5:30 p.m. That's funny, that sounds like the time I'm planning to get there myself. I need to catch the 6:00 train from Munich to Plattling.*

Suddenly I get an uneasy feeling in the pit of my stomach — something's not right here . . .

My eyes jump quickly to the bottom of the sheet, and I gasp when I see that this train that I'm on gets into Munich at 7:05—an hour too late! The awful truth hits me like a fist: I'm supposed to change trains here at Fulda! I've got to get off this train and onto the other one!

I start shoving everything from the tabletop into my knapsack. Pencils, prayer book, paperback, and pretzels all vanish with a sweep of a hand. I'm on my feet, shrugging into my blazer while pulling my suitcase and my winter coat from the overhead rack. I have to get off the train before it pulls out! Any second now it'll start to move, and I'll be in a real mess! With barely a glance at my empty place to see if I've left anything behind, I stagger up the aisle toward the nearest exit. I toss my suitcase ahead of me into the entryway by the open door, hoping that the conductor outside will realize that there's still someone planning to get off. I'm in the vestibule looking down at the conductor who is standing peacefully on the platform, his breath making big puffs of steam in the frosty air. Clutching my suitcase and my knapsack with its half-open zipper, I clamber down the steep steps squeezing my overcoat under one elbow, its collar dragging at my ankles.

I step noiselessly onto the cushion of new snow that carpets the little station platform and ask the conductor if there is indeed an express for Munich due in here in five minutes. "*Ja wohl!*" he assures me. Right on this same track, in fact. I just have to stand right where I am for a few minutes. I thank him as he signals the engineer that all is ready and climbs back up through the doorway. The snow-speckled train glides silently away from the station to continue its journey without me.

I'm alone on the white-blanketed platform whose tiny roof offers little protection from the driving snow. As I turn my overcoat right side up and slip it on, my pulse still racing from the excitement, I hope my frantic calculations were correct. I wonder if the next train really *will* come along and take me to Munich . . .

Over time, the Abbey of Fulda became richer and richer, until by the thirteenth century it owned enough land to become a territorial state, and its abbot held the rank of a Prince of the Holy Roman Empire. By this time only noblemen could be admitted as monks, and Fulda, once famous for its scrupulous observance of monastic discipline, began to grow lax. The monks led a very comfortable existence, hardly appropriate for religious whose founder once wrote that "a monk's life ought always to be a little Lent." They could no longer hear the call to holiness. Although in real need of renewal, the abbey went untouched by the great monastic reforms happening elsewhere in Europe, and the monks continued their worldly ways for a few more decades . . .

A fuzzy point of yellow light appears in the distance, getting larger as it emerges out of the gray afternoon. The familiar throb of a diesel locomotive mixes with the hiss of wind and snow as the Munich-bound express rumbles in right on time. I climb aboard and I work my way down the aisle. I slump into an empty seat, my heart still thumping from my narrow escape.

The colorless white-and-black scenery is sliding by the window again. My pulse starts to slow down at last. I begin to realize what a close call I have just had. *What if I hadn't looked at that schedule when I did? What if I'd waited one more minute before glancing at it?* I had been sitting there quite at ease, with all my things spread out for a long trip, when suddenly I had ten seconds to scoop up all my belongings and beat an undignified retreat.

A saint is always aware of being on a journey that can end at any moment. In this Advent season Jesus has been warning his followers, "You, too, must stand ready, for the Son of Man is coming at an hour you do not expect!"

But what about me? Do I have a lot of unfinished business? Do I owe someone a long-overdue apology? Is there a promise that I still haven't kept, or an act of kindness that I've been postponing? Am I so wrapped up in my everyday work or in my worries that I'm not even thinking much about God or about leaving the train? Sometimes, like those noblemen-monks of Fulda in the 1300s, I can get too distracted or too comfortable, and forget that I'm on a journey to somewhere else. Inevitably, though, someday the Lord is going to say, "Wake up! This is Fulda, and you've got to get off—right now!"

Outside the window night has fallen, and the frozen snowscape of Hesse is rolling past unseen. As the train clacks its way south I pick up the schedule from the seat beside me and double check the arrival time for Munich. Just making sure.

S Cyprien

Working at Low Tide
Muros, Spain

The afternoon bus from La Coruña is weaving its way south down the ragged coast of northwestern Spain. The scenery is a kaleidoscope of mountain slopes, evergreen groves, and rocky seascapes.

Straight ahead spreads a broad blue bay, and, beyond it soar high brown mountains, clad to the waist in dark pine forests. Each isolated house along the narrow road salutes us with a line of bright-colored laundry that flutters sideways in the strong sea wind. Shrunken old ladies in black sit in a row, their backs against the wall of the village church, catching the late afternoon sun. Here and there, a stranded palm tree stands beside the road as if waiting for a ride from a friend. On a headland to our right, a lighthouse pops out of a green meadow like a giant, white thumb. Just off shore, a black fishing boat beetles across the darkening sea. A wide, silver beach peeks playfully from behind the tall straight trunks of a pine grove.

As we round a bend, the next panorama opens up in the distance: lofty gray mountains dotted with greenery encircle a wide cove. White two-story buildings with red tile roofs are strung in a necklace that lies along the road, hugging the horseshoe of the harbor. Their windows face the street and look across it to the waterfront and the bay. Above the row of red roofs, other houses climb the steep granite slope.

Halfway around the horseshoe, the bus drops me off and continues on its way toward Orense. I stand still for a moment to enjoy the smell of the cool sea air. Seagulls skim and soar, scolding the bright-colored fishing boats that are resting at their docks. The quiet, black water sloshes lazily against the rocks lining the shore. This is Muros. I've come here to visit the grandmother of two of my students. I introduced myself to her by phone two days ago, and have now shown up to impose on her hospitality.

A friendly passerby points me toward the street I want. As it turns out, though, the name I give her actually refers to a whole maze of lanes and pathways that crisscross the hillside farther along the curve of the bay. To add to my confusion, house numbers are assigned somewhat haphazardly, and I need the help of a second neighbor woman to locate my destination.

At last I find myself saying hello to the grandmother: "¡Buenas tardes, abuela!" Her daughter, who is visiting from America, soon stops by to say hello and chat. Grandma's generous supper, combined with the salt air and the fatigue of the long bus ride, makes me ready for bed soon after we leave the table. My room is upstairs, at the front of the house. Its window faces the bay, though there's nothing but inky darkness outside when I turn off the light . . .

The harsh cries of the seagulls wake me. A dull, silver dawn is just starting to filter through the little window. Impatient for my first look at the harbor from up here on the hillside I climb out of bed, put on my glasses, and shuffle sleepily across the room, noticing the tangy smell of the sea. As I brush aside the white curtains I blink in disbelief. The bay is gone!

At the bottom of the slope stretches more than half a mile of ugly mud and wet sand. Far out from the shore a tractor and a dump truck slide noiselessly over the brown muck that was water last night. Several men are working busily with rakes and shovels near the truck.

After breakfast I thank *la abuela* and say good-bye for the day. Gray rain clouds are gathering on the horizon as I start down the twisting lanes to inspect the disaster scene at the waterfront. I reach the bottom of the hillside, cross the road and sit down at the edge of the mud on a bench that last evening looked out over silky ripples. And I reflect . . .

For me the "real" Muros is the picturesque one I saw yesterday: the beautiful bay brimming full, its waters lapping at the rocks along the beach front. The bleak sight before me now is some sort of blunder: it's supposed to be a glistening expanse of saltwater, not an unsightly wasteland of dark-brown muck strewn with small boats lying on their sides like dead birds. This isn't the way a fishing port is supposed to look.

The more I get used to the scene, however, the more I start to realize that there is nothing wrong with it at all: this is exactly what Muros is supposed to look like—*when the tide is out!*

My life, it occurs to me, is not so different. It, too, has its high and low tides. I usually see the good times, when life is a joy and the tide is full, as the way life is "*supposed* to be." The other times, when the tide is out, are simply unwanted interruptions. I resent the periods of mud and suffering, and try to just ignore them until they go away.

In a coastal town, though, high tide and low tide are two equally important realities. It's not that one or the other is the way the sea is supposed to be; each one offers its own opportunities. Low tide is the time for clam diggers to go out to find clams, and for mussel farmers to harvest their shellfish from the wooden posts that stand in the sea bed near shore. In the case of Muros, low tide means something else as well: the workers with their tractor and truck, I was told at breakfast, are removing the residue of an oil spill that fouled the coast years before. They take advantage of low tide every day to drive out to the polluted part of the bay floor and clean it up some more. Then, as the tide comes flooding back in, they beat a retreat and wait for the next low water . . .

Heavy clouds are now looming closer every minute. Galicia is famous for its rainy climate. When they hear the word *Gallego* (a Galician), most Spaniards automatically picture someone carrying a furled umbrella, ready for the next shower.

Perhaps, I think, as I look out at the bay, we actually learn more about ourselves when the sea of our life is low than when it is high—because a lot more of the bay is exposed to view. The times of sadness, strain, disappointment, and tragedy let us see certain truths about ourselves that we'd never have noticed otherwise; things about us that need changing stand out especially starkly in the brown mud. It isn't particularly pleasant or pretty, but it is wonderfully useful for making us sinners into saints. It would be a shame to waste this precious time waiting for the next high tide . . .

My supervision of the workmen comes to a sudden halt when a large gray cloud starts to dump the first shower of the day. I quickly unfold my little black umbrella and scurry toward a nearby coffee shop, leaving the low-tide laborers to their cleanup.

Watching Your Valuables
Waterloo, Belgium

The night is as black as licorice. I'm sitting alone in a compartment of the Amsterdam-to-Paris train. I click off the overhead lamp and start watching mysterious pinpoints of light slide past outside. We rumble through little stations whose darkened windows stare like great blind eyes. We're crossing Belgium, that favorite corridor for armies charging back and forth between France and Germany. The constant rhythmic clacking of wheels and rails lulls me to sleep in my seat . . .

I hear distant cannon fire and the whinnying of terrified horses, echoes of the desperate battles of 1914 in the Ardennes forest far to the east. The sharp smell of gunpowder wafts across the hills . . .

I wake up as a weird glaring light comes pouring through the window and paints my compartment with unnatural colors. I hold my hands in front of me, and they glow light blue. We're pulling into the station of some large city. Since we've already passed Antwerp, this is probably Brussels. A handful of quiet figures stand on the concrete platform under the fluorescent lights watching the train come to a stop. There's always something sad about travelers waiting in a station in the middle of the night. The muffled sound of their voices comes through the window. There are a couple of anonymous thumps out in the corridor as suitcases bump against the walls. A shrill whistle from the conductor, and a moment later we glide out of the station. In a few minutes we'll pass near the town of Waterloo south of Brussels. I doze off . . .

Napoleon's troops are scurrying about, preparing for a charge across a flat plain at first light. Drums roll, calling the soldiers to form ranks behind their banners. In the morning mist the Duke of Wellington's English are already awaiting the fateful attack . . .

I sense a human presence in the compartment with me. I half open my eyes to see a man in a suit and tie sitting in the shadows on the opposite side of the dark compartment, just inside the sliding door. Funny, he came in without making a sound. My senses are dull with sleep, and my head is heavy on my shoulders. Soon my cheek rests once again against the rough cloth of the window curtain and my eyelids droop closed . . .

The battle trumpet sounds, the drums pound, and the attack begins. The French troops charge across the wide field. Horses snort and neigh in the heat of battle. The cannons belch death and mutilation into the enemy's charging lines . . .

I sense that presence again, but nearer this time. I open my eyes a little and am startled to see that the man in the suit is now standing just a few inches away from me, to my right, his arms stretching up over my head. His hands are busy on the luggage shelf above me.

The little part of my brain that doesn't go to sleep on trains gives the rest of me a poke and asks, "Why is this man standing here reaching up to the overhead rack where your blazer is?" In an instant my eyes are wide open. I tilt my head up toward the dark form hovering above me and ask in polite, sleepy French, "Can I help you?" He doesn't answer, but instead just calmly turns to his left, takes two or three steps back to his corner seat by the door and sits down . . .

My eyelids close once more . . .

I hear a familiar sound: the door to the corridor is slowly sliding shut. The corner seat is empty, and I'm alone in the compartment again. It's 2:05 a.m. As the clouds clear from my brain I start to realize that my visitor had been going through my coat pockets looking for my wallet!

I'm not awake enough to be angry at him, but I have to admire his nerve. Then I start to scold myself for not being more aware that something unusual was afoot. This stranger shows up in my compartment looking for a seat a full half-hour after we left the last station. How could I have been so slow to pick up on that?

Finally I end up feeling insulted. Did that guy really think that I would be dumb enough to leave anything of value lying around where some stranger could just sneak in and snatch it? In fact, when I'm on a night train, I always put my passport, wallet and tickets in my back pocket and sit on them. (This is not very comfortable, but it's highly effective.) The thief, then, never had the slightest chance of stealing anything of value from me. Now wide awake, I realize that I've just had a good lesson in the virtue of watchfulness.

Saints don't need to be paranoid, of course; but we do need to watch out for the forces in our lives that can slowly weaken our commitment to living the Gospel. Like my night visitor, these influences often slip in quietly.

There is, for example, our natural tendency to think and act like everyone else around us. If coffee-break banter is always snickering gossip, we may gradually forget that unkind speech is a dangerous sin against community. If others show off their success with expensive new cars or homes, we may find that our own sense of Christian moderation with regard to money is weakening.

And there is also the mass media. TV sitcoms and junk magazines slip into our homes dressed in the latest fashion, and soon we think of them as old friends. We put double locks on our doors and burglar alarms on our windows, but, in rented movies and TV, we welcome into our homes a parade of seedy strangers—strangers who are reshaping our deepest beliefs and convictions.

Materialism, deceit, selfishness, and promiscuity: often repeated and so attractively packaged, these messages of the mass media are tremendously powerful. Constant and indiscriminate exposure to them will inevitably change our attitudes, confuse our sense of right and wrong, and weaken our determination to follow Christ.

The saint is not alone in the train compartment. Lots of characters are always passing in and out—and some of them bear careful watching! On the long night's journey to the Kingdom there has to be a part of me that doesn't go to sleep, that asks questions: "Why am I watching a music video that shows women as clinging sexual objects?" "Would I be buying this if the rest of the crowd were not?" The saint must keep shooing off the well-dressed night visitors: "Excuse me! Can I help you?". . .

Lines of German Panzer tanks are rolling past my window to join the furious fighting in eastern Belgium. It's 1944, and General Dwight Eisenhower's troops are digging in for a fight to the death. History will call it "The Battle of the Bulge." Clouds of oily black smoke billow from burning towns on the horizon. It's as if the sky itself were on fire over there . . .

Then I realize that the red in the sky is the sunrise. The smoke is just city smog hanging over the Parisian suburbs. I stand up and stretch my arms over my head with a short grunt, swaying as the train clatters and lurches on its final few miles. I notice, just above eye-level, my navy blue blazer lying in its place on the rack. My right hand reaches back instinctively to tap my pants pocket. I smile smugly as I feel passport and wallet still safe where they belong.

Outside the window the distant white domes of Sacré Coeur Basilica glow pink in the dawn over Paris.

Cloître ~ S. Trophime, Arles

Cleaning Up Your Image
Arles, France

I park my rented car in a lot near the ancient Roman arena in Arles and set off on foot through the narrow, picturesque streets. This delightful town of gray stone buildings and orange tile roofs is famous for its well-preserved Roman ruins.

Located at the delta where the Rhone empties into the Mediterranean, Arelatae, as the Romans called it, was once the second capital of the Roman world. The partially restored amphitheater and the coliseum-like arena are both still used for special events today. Their immense size and sober dignity are a pleasant contrast to the lighthearted spirit of present-day Arles.

It was in a college art class that I first saw pictures of the lovely carved portal that graces the front of the church of St. Trophime, one of the great treasures of Romanesque architecture. This morning I'm finally going to be able to just stand there and marvel at it with my own eyes. Then, right beside the church, there will be the famous cloister garden, the most beautiful one in southern France.

Arriving at last in the wide, stone-paved Place de la République, I immediately turn to my left, toward the facade of St. Trophime. After a wait of more than thirty years, I am finally able to stand here in person and look up at—four stories of scaffolding! The famous carved Romanesque doorway is completely hidden behind ugly panels of corrugated steel! I stand and stare in angry disbelief for a few moments, and then, heavy with disappointment, I shuffle halfheartedly into the church.

Since it's not yet nine o'clock in the morning, I have it all to myself. I sit and pray for a while in the quiet glow of the early sun beneath towering twelfth-century vaults topped with rounded Romanesque arches. My guidebook calls the interior "the high point of Romanesque church architecture." I turn the page and look wistfully at a color photograph of the famous portal that I won't get to see. It's a set of pillars arranged like a triumphal arch, symbolizing the entrance of the People of God into the Heavenly Jerusalem. It includes beautifully carved stone statues of saints and, in the semicircular tympanum above the main doors, the famous scene of "Christ in Judgment." I have to admit that even in this flattering photograph the whole thing is blackened and filthy with the soot of centuries. I imagine how glorious it will look after a good cleaning.

I walk out of the church through the forest of scaffold pipes and plywood panels and back onto the plaza. A few yards to the left, I step through the entrance of St. Trophime's cloister garden. I sense right away the gentle peacefulness of the place, a sort of timeless hush, as if the pewter-colored stones were absorbing all the sounds of the world. I follow the arcaded stone walkway that surrounds the square patch of bright green lawn. On two of the four sides Romanesque columns with squat little sculptures on the capitals support rounded arches. Along the other two sides the pointed gothic arches display carvings that are more intricate and elegant. The cloister garden keeps the easy quietness it had when the canons of St. Trophime, who followed the Rule of St. Augustine, used this as their place of meditation and prayer.

I sit down on a stone bench and take out a photocopy of a Latin sermon written by Caesarius of Arles, a favorite saint of mine. I've brought it all the way from my monastery back home just so I can sit here and enjoy it in the town where it was written. Caesarius was bishop here for forty years around the year 500, long before this church or cloister were built. He had been a monk of the monastery of Lérins on the island of St. Honorat near Cannes, but then was sent here to Arles to be its bishop. He became famous as a preacher, a theologian, and a saint.

I unfold the sermon, which has traveled so far to come back to its home. As usual, Caesarius's Latin is not the richly ornate language of Augustine (which I find too hard to read), but is deliberately simple and homespun, intended to reach the common people. This sermon is on one of his favorite subjects: the dangers posed by "little" sins, those daily faults that are a normal part of life.

One reason they're dangerous is that we are in a battle with an enemy; there's no room for letting down one's guard. People who figure that they're safe because they don't have any grave sins are likely to get overconfident. "It is exactly at this point that you get seriously wounded because you are not expecting the attack."

"Some of you," the bishop warns, "are misled into thinking that just because you never do anything evil, God will surely judge you worthy of everlasting life." I think of the elegant carving of Christ in Judgment that is hidden by the workmen's scaffold. "Well, let me remind you of Jesus' parable about the last judgment: the tree gets cut down and thrown into the fire not for bearing _bad_ fruit but for bearing _no_ fruit." If you haven't been about the business of bearing the fruit of love and forgiveness, the bishop warns, then you'd better start right now!

Caesarius shows his characteristic impatience with people who are satisfied with just being "pretty good," who have made an easy truce with their daily faults and petty vices. I squirm a bit on the stone bench as he brings up the example of Ananias who was struck dead for holding back just a small part of what he had promised to give to the Lord. God isn't interested in having *most* of what I have—God wants it *all!*

I remember another sermon, in which Caesarius points out to some monks how illogical it is to join the monastery and then be lukewarm in living the monastic life. Why pay the high price of giving up all the pleasures of the world so as to be free to follow Christ and then, once in the monastery, be only halfhearted about it? Before being made a bishop, Caesarius had been the "cellarer" of the monastery of Lérins, in charge of distributing supplies and daily necessities to the monks. They say he was removed from that job because he was too strict in dealing with his brethren. Reading his sermons, I can believe it.

Black birds dart and swoop in tight circles, playing an irreverent game of tag above the dusty orange tiles of the church roof . . .

Caesarius's relentless demands for holiness, however, spring from this fundamental optimistic belief: we are made in the image of God. The image is often tarnished or caked with layers of "*parvas negligentias quotidianas,*" daily little faults. After years of neglect, it can get to be so covered over as to be unrecognizable. I think of the blackened portal of St. Trophime nearby. Removing those layers and letting our true self shine through takes constant care and the regular practice of prayer, penance, and almsgiving. The bishop encourages and scolds his hearers: *Hey! You can do better than that! After all, you're the image of God!* I may be satisfied with leaving a little dirt on the image, but my bishop friend clearly is not . . .

When I finish reading I stand up and stretch, squinting into the warm summer sun. Reluctantly, I fold up the pages of the sermon and tuck them back into my knapsack.

Leaving the gray stone arches, the rich green grass, and the tranquil silence, I walk out of the cloister garden into the busy Place de la République. As I pass in front of the scaffold hiding the church, I hear the voices of the workers who are painstakingly removing years of dirt. After several more months all of the holy images will be restored to their original beauty, thanks to the thorough cleaning. *Yes,* I think to myself, *Caesarius would definitely approve.*

Breaking Chains
Toledo, Spain

I'm strolling toward the old part of Toledo from the bus terminal well outside the ancient walls. In A.D.123 Titus Livy described Toledo as "a small fortified city." Since that time, it has changed hands among Romans, Visigoths, Moslems, and Spanish monarchs. On this spring morning as I approach the city gate, Toledo still keeps its air of "a small fortified city."

I recognize the familiar skyline from the famous painting *Storm Over Toledo*, El Greco's almost mystical vision of the cathedral on the hilltop, its gray tower pointing into the shreds of black and silver cloud as vibrant green fields in the foreground climb upward toward the purplish-gray city walls. I pass through the medieval gate and start to explore the ramparts, the immense cathedral, and the narrow streets whose houses bear the stamp of 360 years of Moslem rule.

After wandering around for some hours I find myself in a wide sun-bathed plaza beside the monastery church of San Juan de los Reyes. High up on an outside wall, hanging in neat rows, are curious ironwork objects about a foot-and-a-half long. A minute of riffling through my guidebook answers my question: these are ankle chains taken off of Christian slaves freed from the Moslems by the victorious Spaniards in 1492. I sit down on a bench to study these grisly reminders of slavery, and suddenly I am struck by how well they seem to fit there . . .

What more appropriate trophies for Christians than the broken chains of their former captivity? And what better place to display such trophies than on the side of a church?

God became flesh, suffered, died, and rose again to free us from the chains of sin and death. We are no longer slaves to evil, doubt, and despair, because the Lord has loosed our bonds. God is in the business of breaking chains.

The wall of San Juan de los Reyes glowing in the afternoon sun easily becomes the wall of my own Abbey Church. The rusting Moslem leg irons suddenly belong not to anonymous slaves, but to me and my brother monks back home and to our parishioners and students. The broken shackles become souvenirs of temptations we've overcome, trophies of little triumphs over vices, the tally of the times Jesus' saving power has set someone free.

What if the eyes of faith were allowed to see trophies displayed like this on every church wall in the world? What if every victory over the fetters of pettiness and jealousy, for example, were recorded by hanging up the broken chains somewhere as an encouragement for the rest of us? What if we could actually see and count up the hundreds, thousands, and millions of times that Jesus has delivered some Christian's heart from the slavery of pride, hatred, or racial prejudice? What if we decorated the walls of schools and colleges with the broken bonds of ignorance overcome? What if the walls of drug and alcohol treatment centers could display to the world the proud trophies of victories over chemical dependence? What if houses and apartment buildings were decked with the rusty remains of family misunderstandings that have been overcome by love, courage, and God's grace? What an encouragement to people who know they are called to holiness but find themselves still struggling with weaknesses, sins, or addictions! The display of shattered chains in front of me this afternoon prompts me to steal a glance at my own personal chains—the broken ones and the unbroken.

Perhaps just as important, though, is the reminder that the call to be a saint is the call to be a chain-breaker. *Making* chains is much easier, of course—I can do it without even trying. It only takes an unkind remark toward a person to tighten around his or her ankles the chains of a poor self-image. It only takes a racial or ethnic joke to tighten around my hearer's ankles the chains of prejudice or racism. Merely speaking about money or possessions in a certain way in front of children is a great way to strengthen shackles of materialism around them. The rusted pieces of iron hanging on the church wall in Toledo remind all saints of their responsibility.

It's time to step back out of El Greco's painting and into the reality of evening traffic and long lines at the bus station. On my walk down the hill, I spot another church, but there are no chains on the wall. I start looking for them everywhere: on houses, bars, and police stations. I can almost see one, I think, in the shadow underneath that balcony, where an old woman is sitting in the doorway, watching the sun go down.

Paris — St Eustache   10

Part Four
Holiness 101

AUBRAC

Listening

Aubrac, France

My feet are sore. I've been following the red-and-white trail markers for several hilly miles. They have led me along muddy cow paths, beside rough stone walls and barbed-wire fences, through thick woods, and across lush meadows in the rugged uplands of central France. I'm alone except for an occasional fellow-hiker and a few friendly cows who ignore me as I tiptoe uneasily across their pasture within a few feet of them. The hiking trail, officially called "GR-65," follows a path worn by thousands of medieval pilgrims. They were walking the 800 miles from LePuy in France to Santiago de Compostela in northwestern Spain to venerate the relics of Saint James the Apostle. Under a bleak, threatening sky, I'm making my own pilgrim way to the town of Aubrac with my mind on those hearty predecessors who trudged hundreds of dangerous, weary miles to fulfill their pilgrimage vows.

At last, from the top of a grassy hill, I spot a lazy little village loafing in a patch of sunlight a couple of miles ahead. That must be Aubrac: a cluster of gray granite buildings and a few tall green trees. It looks out of place, as if some careless giant has dropped it into the middle of the rolling meadows by mistake.

I flop down beside the path to rest my feet and to make a sketch of the tiny town. Its monastery and surrounding wall are gone, as are most of the other original buildings. Only a couple of sturdy, stone two-story inns, a low Romanesque church, and the "Tower of the English" remain.

Behind me I can hear the ghostly footfalls of pious phantom travelers on their way to Compostela, and I no longer feel alone.

When my sketch is finished, I stand up, dust myself off, shoulder my knapsack and pick up the trail again as it winds its way down the sloping meadows toward Aubrac. The church steeple disappears behind a hill and pops up once more a few minutes later. Then it hides a second time, only to reappear in a couple of moments. My feet start to ache again. To take my mind off the soreness I start telling myself the story of Aubrac . . .

In the 1200s, a Flemish knight was making the difficult pilgrimage from LePuy westward toward Compostela. Early on he had to cross the wilds of this plateau of Aubrac. He was waylaid by robbers on his outward journey across the uninhabited uplands. Then, on his return trip, he was suddenly engulfed in a freak blizzard. The knight made a vow that if he arrived home safely from his perilous trip he would have a way station built halfway across the Aubrac wilderness to help the pilgrims who were to come after him. The present hamlet of Aubrac proves that he was a man of his word. The order of Knights Hospitallers founded a priory here which would grow to be a sizable cluster of about a dozen buildings. While some of these religious men were offering lodging and food to the travelers, others, knights on horseback, would ride through the countryside hunting down robbers.

The squat church steeple pops into view again. That must be the home of Maria.

Her full name is *Maria, la Cloche des Perdus,* "Maria, the Lost People's Bell." Every evening around sundown, the bell was tolled for two hours to guide wayfarers who were still out on the pilgrim trail, caught by the sudden onset of darkness. Whenever there was a heavy fog or a bad storm that made traveling more dangerous than usual, Maria sang out at regular intervals to act as a sort of homing device for unfortunate travelers wandering out on the uplands. Anyone lost in the wilderness could just listen for the bell and then follow the sound to the safety of the town.

Nowadays most of us lead lives that are so busy that we can easily lose our bearings. We, too, can look up only to realize that darkness is falling unexpectedly.

When we have to deal with tremendous demands from family, job, and so on, the pilgrim saints of Aubrac have a lesson for us: the travelers crossing these hazardous uplands realized the value of *silence.* They knew that to find their way through the fog or the dark, they needed to listen for that bell. It was hard to hear Maria above the roar of wind and rain, so the trick was to stand still, be quiet, and listen very hard. After a while, they would begin to catch faint whispers of her voice riding on the wind, and that would be enough to guide them in the right direction through the storm.

Christian spiritual tradition has always known the value of frequent quiet prayer, of "resting in God." We need to be connected with the world of silence where God dwells, deep down in our innermost selves. In the expectant quiet of prayer and meditation, the voice of the Spirit of truth speaks to us from within. Of course, silence can be scary. It's even scarier when the voice that speaks out of the quiet tells us something we don't want to hear, such as a truth about ourselves that we've been unwilling to deal with. Maybe the bell will tell us we're heading off in the wrong direction and then we'll have to change our lives. No wonder so many people try to fill every moment with noise—they're afraid that they might hear the sound of the bell calling them to turn around.

Most of the saints lead lives that are filled with the unpredictable demands of caring for their children, working on their marriages, holding down a job, and trying to keep in touch with friends and relatives. Through no fault of their own, "quiet time" has become a rare luxury.

Sometimes we find that despite our best efforts, our day is filled with people, deadlines, and jobs that require a lot of concentration. Even then, however, we can learn to listen, through the roar of wind and rain, for the bell. We can turn off the car radio or the CD player or the television. Once we learn the value of quiet, it's amazing how much of it we can actually find.

Sometimes the sound of the bell can help you to correct your course. A coworker marches toward me with a telltale look in her eye, and I steel myself. *She's probably going to try to blame me for that fiasco at the meeting this morning. Well, just let her try. She'll get an earful—* Then the woman walks past. She wasn't coming to see me at all! But I was ready to be ugly with her. That's the sound of the distant bell telling me that I'm getting off the path.

A teenage son comes up to his mother and spontaneously offers, "I'll be happy to baby-sit for a while if you need to go grocery shopping." Shocked, she begins to pray: "Sometimes, Jesus, just when I think I've been a total failure with that kid, he does something like this! Thank you for the encouragement! You must have known I needed it!" The sound of the bell is coming through over the shouts from the playroom and the rock music on the radio upstairs, assuring her that she is on the right path . . .

The trail has now joined a paved road. I can make out the mustard-colored moss on the church wall and a red bicycle leaning against the side of a house. I can almost feel the presence of the Hospitallers who once made this a safe haven for the weary pilgrim.

On my left are the Tower of the English and the little church with its bell tower. I notice an old stone inn farther down the road on the right. The friendly smoke curling from its chimney draws me, hungry and thirsty, to its door. Aubrac at last!—and my feet have stopped hurting.

Hoping

Loch Ness, Scotland

All morning, the cold rain has been crackling against the dark windowpane of the guest room in the monastery of Fort Augustus. This afternoon I'm glad for the invitation to climb the stairs of the abbey's bell tower with a brother who has to change the measurement card in the sunlight recorder. (The Royal Weather Service once reported that this village has the fewest hours of sunshine per year of any town in the United Kingdom!) We're on the narrow stone steps that wind steeply upward inside the square tower. I clutch the hem of my black Benedictine habit in one hand to keep from tripping on it, and I start remembering what I've read about the geology of these Scottish highlands.

Between three and four hundred million years ago, in a succession of tremors, Scotland cracked open along a diagonal fault running across the whole island from northeast to southwest. The northern part slowly slid southwest some sixty-five miles. Then, more recently (somewhere between ten and twenty-five thousand years ago), glaciers four thousand feet thick scoured the open wound and shaped it into what is called on the map "The Great Glen." Today the Glen includes a lake twenty-two miles long, a mile-and-a-half wide at its widest, and 700 feet deep for most of its length. Tree-clad mountains rise 2,000 feet on either side of this, the largest freshwater lake in Great Britain and the third deepest in Europe. This is Loch Ness.

At the southwestern end of the Loch, where the River Oich empties in, lies the hamlet of Fort Augustus. In the 1700s, the English king put a fort here to control the clans and subdue the proud Highlanders. On the site today stands the Benedictine monastery of Fort Augustus Abbey where I'm staying for the week. It's this monastery's tower that I'm climbing right now.

We're at the top of the stairs already. While the good brother sets about replacing the little cardboard disc in the sunlight recorder inside the tower, I step through a low doorway and out onto the walkway that circles the tower high above Loch Ness. I rest my elbows on the rough stone parapet and take in the scene below.

The rain has stopped, except for an occasional stray drop that glints in the fickle sunlight. Gray, frayed clouds and a few tattered rags of blue sky hang over the brooding black of the Loch. Steep mountainsides of gold, brown, green, and burgundy stretch quietly along both sides of the narrow lake to disappear in the dim distance. Straight ahead, in the center of the scene, arching up out of the dark waters of Loch Ness in a gorgeous glimmering curve of colors, glows a shiny new rainbow. Like most really bright rainbows, this one almost seems to be giving off a quiet hum.

Everything is hushed except for the whisper of the rainbow and the whistle of the winter wind flapping my cassock around my knees. I'm struck by the unlikely contrast: the murky, mist-shrouded ink of Loch Ness and the sparkling colors of the rainbow.

The Loch is famous for only one thing nowadays, of course—the notorious monster that shows itself every now and then, just often enough to keep scientists, writers, and tourists busy speculating. After breakfast this morning, Old Father Gregory told me that he and a friend saw "Nessie" from the monastery's dock in 1971. The dark waters of Loch Ness have become a symbol of unsolved mystery: somewhere in their depths lurks a creature left over from the first days of creation when God made the sea monsters.

The story of the rainbow, like that of the creation of the sea monsters, goes back to the Book of Genesis. God has finished the work of creating the world, bringing order out of the primordial chaos, and sees that it is good. Then, not long afterward, the forces of disorder reenter the picture. There are signs that the order of creation is breaking down: the disobedience of Adam and Eve in eating of the forbidden fruit; the murder of Abel by his own brother, Cain; and the arrogant raising of the Tower of Babel toward heaven. Then, with the coming of the great flood, the world is finally plunged back into complete chaos. When the waters have receded, Noah steps out of the ark, and God speaks to him, promising that never again will the dark powers of evil be allowed to overwhelm the earth. As the sign and the guarantee of the divine promise the Lord fashions something brand-new, a sort of supplement to the work of creation: the rainbow. This, the only thing God is said to have created outside the first six days, the Lord now places like a "bow in the clouds." To this day, the rainbow is our assurance that God will always control the forces of darkness, disorder, and chaos that keep trying to destroy our world.

You have to be in the right place at the right time to see a rainbow. First, you have to be in or near a rainstorm, under dark clouds. Second, you can't be facing the sun, enjoying its warmth on your face, but must have your back to it. It's a perfect sign of hope, a gift for people who are overshadowed by rain clouds in their lives, who are experiencing showers of discouragement, despair, or depression. It only appears to people who, for whatever reason, aren't looking toward the light. Perhaps they don't know the right direction, or maybe they're angry and have turned their back on God. But it is then that they are candidates for a rainbow.

This winter rainbow leaps out of Loch Ness the way hope springs up in the midst of a painful mystery. The joyful bundle of light curves up from the murky Loch like new confidence suddenly bursting out of the depths of an unfathomable problem. The sunlight bounces off the raindrops the way God's love sometimes shines through our tears to make a beautiful bow in the clouds, God's "I promise" holding good in the face of our personal chaos. A saint knows that the rainbow always appears sooner or later. Sometimes it seems late in coming, sometimes it's very faint, sometimes only a piece of it can be seen. But a saint is skillful in finding rainbows in clouds—maybe because a saint is one who knows for certain that the rainbow is there somewhere?

"Well, Father! The sunshine recorder is reset. Oh, I say! You're looking a bit cold! Ready to come back inside?" It's my meteorologist guide popping his head out of the door. "Yes, thanks," I answer, stealing a last glance at the lake before I follow him inside.

Dieppe.
Le Château

Balancing

Dieppe, France

Sitting as she does at the water's edge on the rugged Normandy coastline, Dieppe is constantly having her hair blown back by the winds that whip across the English Channel. From my cliff-top vantage point I can see that her streets are laid out and the gates in her old town walls placed in such a way as to reduce the effect of the constant sea breeze. At our feet, a charming little castle, perched solidly atop a rocky knob, looks out across the Channel.

Beyond the castle, in the center of the scene, a great grassy esplanade runs right along the water's edge, separating the front row of the town's buildings on the right from the beach on the left. Ancient engravings show that this same broad field, several blocks long and a hundred yards wide, has changed very little over the passing centuries. Despite the low clouds heavy with threatening rain, the green meadow is especially crowded today. Tugging impatiently against their invisible strings, dozens of bright-colored kites are riding the steady wind. The stiff breeze holds them almost motionless, their tails pointing straight inland toward the roofs and steeples of town. There are box kites of red and white, cylinder kites of yellow and orange, a green kite that looks like a quilted saltine, and a couple that seem like big blue rubber rafts floating on an unseen sea.

The perpetual breeze makes the beachfront park a favorite spot for kite-fliers all year round, and this week Dieppe is the proud host of an international kite-fliers' convention. Her skies are alive with colorful kites, and her streets teem with folks from Asia, the Americas, Africa, Australia, and Europe who share a passion for building and flying them.

I have the good luck to get invited to the official reception for the participants at the *hôtel de ville*, Dieppe's modern town hall. The speeches include many references to the beautiful harmony of nations among the participants engaged in such an innocent, childlike exercise of the spirit. While the various foreign delegations are presenting their symbolic gifts to the mayor, a question keeps pushing to the front of my mind: *Are these people serious?* On the one hand, they are clearly in earnest, because this kind of kiting involves a real commitment of time, money, and energy. On the other hand, these grown men and women spend hours standing in fields holding strings and watching their pretty-colored playthings slide and glide in the breeze.

As the ceremony continues, I realize that kite-flying is neither serious nor playful; it's . . . *spoudogeloios!*

I came across this tongue-twisting adjective from classical Greek many years ago, and we've been friends ever since. It's a combination of two words: *spoudos*, "serious, earnest," and *gelein*, "to laugh." So *spoudogeloios* means something like "grave-merry" or "serious-playful." For the ancient Greeks, the ideal person is one who is poised between the earnest and the playful, who travels through life with the evenness of spirit that comes from balancing heaviness and lightness. If you are *spoudogeloios* you don't take yourself too seriously, yet you appreciate the deep and eternal dimension of the human situation and strive to live accordingly.

It seems to me that this is a marvelous description of Christian holiness: The saint is one who manages to keep the serious and the playful in balance.

There is a light side to Christianity. Our Scriptures are full of "good news." The victory has already been won. "If God is for us, who can be against us?" "I am with you always; yes, to the end of time." "You have turned my mourning into dancing." St. Irenaeus once spoke of the spiritual life as "a divine children's game."

There is also, however, a "heavy" side to our life of faith. The Scriptures are full of grave passages, too: "Keep sober and alert, because your enemy the devil is on the prowl . . ." "Go away from me, with your curse upon you, to the eternal fire . . . for I was hungry and you never gave me food . . ." "For it is not against human enemies that we have to struggle, but against . . . the spirits of evil in the heavens."

A Christian needs to balance the heavy and the light, like a kite that feels both the string tugging it to earth and the wind lifting it off toward the stars.

Some of us are too grim in our relationship with God, treating life as a deadly-serious, white-knuckled, and humorless project. These "heavy" believers just can't lighten up. Their Christianity is all about sin, long faces, and eternal damnation. Their kites are too heavy to fly.

Some of us, on the other hand, are too casual about our life in the spirit. Some people want a God who makes no demands on them, but who is like some pleasant neighbor promising the children ice cream and cookies. They avoid any talk about sin, self-discipline, or the need to deal with the potentially destructive forces at work in the inner self. Their kites are not anchored in the sober truth of the gospel and its demands for constant conversion. They go flying away on the breeze completely out of touch with reality.

Balancing the serious and the playful, the light and the heavy, is a skill that only comes with practice. It takes time to arrive at wisdom, to become *spoudogeloios*, to become a saint. This is why older folks, who have been at it for a long while, usually give the best example of balance. They've learned how to avoid the extremes of heaviness and lightness, and live suspended serenely between heaven and earth . . .

The ceremony ends with a typical French offering of champagne and hors d'oeuvres. As I elbow my way among the Japanese, the Australians, and the Samoans, all talking (I presume) about their kites, I try not to spill my champagne. I ask the Lord to give me a little more of the delightful balance I see among these playful-serious people. Or, even better, the gracefulness of one of their colorful kites as it floats easily in the happy tension between the unseen string and the invisible wind.

S. Severin - Paris

Being Whole

St. Gervais, Paris

The Church of Saints Gervais et Protase stands in the *Marais*, one of the oldest neighborhoods in Paris. The church that formerly stood on this spot was a favorite of Saint Germain, Bishop of Paris about the year 550. King Louis XIII laid the foundation stone for the present building in 1616. This is the first time I've been inside, so, without being too obvious, I try to steal a peek at the great gothic church while I wait for Midday Prayer to begin. Round gray pillars shoot out of the stone floor and zoom straight skyward. In the shadows far overhead, they curve gently until they join one another in a riot of points and arches.

My mind wanders to a wedding held in this very place 378 years ago. The groom is Monsieur Antoine le Gras, and the bride is Mademoiselle Louise de Marillac. She will be a good and faithful wife to him. She will also become a great help to Saint Vincent de Paul, and, after the death of her husband, will be an invaluable coworker in Vincent's great works of charity. Louise will eventually be canonized Saint Louise de Marillac.

Kneeling on the floor of the large chapel located behind the main altar, I feel conspicuous in my black habit—the others around me are wearing white choir robes. Even more unusual is the fact that half of these people are women.

I'm a guest of the monastic "Community of Jerusalem," a group founded in Paris in the 1970s to witness to God's presence in the center of the city. They make a special point of welcoming people to the church of St. Gervais for prayers and mass, and of being available to visitors for spiritual conversation or sympathetic listening. Some hold jobs outside the monastery—one sister, for example works as a medical professional—and others help run the community's bookstore and gift shop. The women live in one house and the men in another three blocks away, and everyone gathers for common worship several times a day.

A bell rings, and we all stand to sing the traditional opening words of the Church's Liturgy of the Hours—"*Dieu, viens à mon aide! Seigneur, à notre secours!*" "O God, come to my assistance, O Lord, make haste to help us!" The voices of forty monastic singers fill the chapel.

When the hymn follows, I'm overwhelmed, almost intoxicated, by the beautiful harmony. Every day for over thirty years I've heard men singing the Liturgy of the Hours, and I've often heard women's voices praising God, too. But the rich sound of men and women chanting in harmony is a new experience.

From the very first chord, this hymn evokes in me a single overwhelming image: *completeness.* Each person contributes his or her natural voice—the light soprano, the colorful mezzo, the meditative alto, the energetic tenor, the full-bodied baritone and the rumbling bass. The high voices blend with low, the heavy with the light, and the dark with the bright. The result is a single beautiful sound of praise.

Certain ancient creation myths (including, it seems, the one in the second chapter of Genesis) tell of how, in the distant past, the original human being somehow got severed into two parts, one male and the other female. This explains why to this day men and women are attracted to each other: they are in reality two halves of one person. Modern psychologists have rediscovered the great truth that underlies this myth. They talk about our psyche as being "androgynous," composed of both masculine and feminine elements at the same time, with the masculine predominating in the male and the feminine side in the female. Once, when I said in class, "You know, every male has a certain amount of the feminine in him," one student, much to the amusement of his classmates, growled defensively "Not me, man! There's nothing feminine about *me!*" I couldn't blame him for being so threatened, given our culture's distorted ideas about what it means to be a "real" man.

The voices now join in chanting a psalm, once again in a simple but full harmony . . .

This music reminds me that each of us can be fully ourselves when and only when the masculine and the feminine are integrated in us. The health of our psyche depends on the fruitful presence of both sides, each contributing to the whole.

Louise and Vincent are two interesting examples of Saints who discover tremendous holiness by developing inner gifts that aren't considered typical of their sex.

Louise de Marillac is very much a woman, well acquainted with the niceties of Parisian society. But in working with St. Vincent de Paul and directing her order of sisters in the care of countless orphans and invalids, she finds another side of herself. She integrates her other side into her personality, putting her aggressiveness and cool-headed organizational ability to work in the service of the poor by organizing the distribution of clothing and food and directing the new order, the Daughters of Charity.

Vincent de Paul, on the other hand, is a man's man. He knows how to get things done, and rubs elbows easily with some of the most powerful figures in France. His friends tell us that he is quick-tempered by nature, and he himself admits that without God's grace he would be "repulsive, rough and cross." He will become the great champion saint of the poor, however, only when he develops his compassionate, gentle, sensitive, nurturing side. Statues often show him with his arms tenderly protecting a couple of orphan children, like a mother hen with her chicks.

Another psalm, this one in a Byzantine harmony where the dark bass line gives a richness to the rest . . .

Vincent de Paul and Louise de Marillac give us a shining example of fruitful collaboration. Each of them brings extraordinary gifts to their partnership, and each benefits from the encouragement and giftedness of the other. All the saints, particularly the poor of the world, still enjoy the fruits of this beautiful cooperation.

Everyone kneels down again for a moment of silent prayer . . .

I pray that I can find the receptive, gentle, mothering side of myself that will make me a more sensitive and caring monk, priest, teacher, colleague, and friend.

I find myself praying for the Church, too, and for all the saints, that we may learn, as Louise and Vincent did, to appreciate one another's gifts and collaborate in preaching the Gospel message in all its beauty and fullness.

We stand, and the prayer service comes to an end with an oration. As we file quietly out of the chapel and into the main body of the church I notice some of the sisters and brothers whispering warm greetings to various people who are waiting for a word with them. I walk through the rear door and out into the sunlight. After crossing a busy street I head down the quiet cobblestones of the narrow rue du Grenier Sur l'Eau. I keep feeling in my soul those rich, healing harmonies of male and female. It's as if I'm listening to a distant echo of the divine music that welled up and overflowed from the very heart of God on the first morning in Eden.

Thanksgiving
Saint Malo, France

Père Michel, the local parish priest, is giving me an evening tour of the narrow streets of his native Saint Malo. This small port town is a peninsula wrapped in twelve hundred meters of stone ramparts and fifteen centuries of sea lore. Her sturdy houses of tan granite, with their steeply pitched slate roofs and dormer windows, tower above the tops of the battlements as if watching the fishing boats in the bay. Due west, over the horizon, is Great Britain.

Saint Malo is a seafarers' city whose intrepid explorers and merchants sailed their three-masted *Cap-horniers* to every part of the globe. They brought back goods and tall tales from Africa and Antarctica, New Orleans and New Zealand, China and Argentina. This is the home port of Jacques Cartier, who set off from here on his first voyage of exploration to Canada in 1534.

Inside the town walls this evening, the smell of the sea and the romance of the sailing days still reach into every corner. My priest-guide, who is practicing his English on me, keeps up an interesting monologue about the history of his town. In the late 1600s, he tells me, corsairs from St. Malo put to sea in their light, swift ships to wreak havoc on English shipping in the name of the king of France. In their heyday, they once captured 3,800 commercial vessels in the space of ten years. It's no wonder the English called Saint Malo a "hornet's nest."

We're now strolling through a corner of the town where the buildings date back to those days. You can still see five-story houses of wood and stone, with bizarre angles at their corners. Crooked chimneys, topped with quaint red chimney pots, sprout up randomly in a rolling sea of slate roofs. Up and down the eight-foot wide streets, the old houses lean into one another in charming disorder, as if jostling and kidding together. Space was already at a premium even back when these houses were built, so they were made high and narrow, with stingy spiral staircases inside and narrow air shafts for ventilation and sunlight. Residents of these wooden buildings slept with their fingers crossed, knowing that the shops and warehouses next door on either side were bulging with tallow, tar, and gunpowder for the tall ships.

I'm now under the spell of Père Michel's stories. My fellow tourists start to look like rough sailors, leathery old sea captains, unsavory barmaids, and swaggering corsairs. They're shouting to one another about the latest exploits of Duguay-Trouin, the first great corsair captain, who has just captured a dozen more English ships this week. I smell pots of molten tar and the smoke from wood chip fires used to treat the bottoms of the ships. Busy merchant establishments, ship chandlers, and taverns are all crowded together along the stinking, muddy streets.

The priest stops at a small wooden door, takes out a key, and lets us through. We begin to wind our way along dark, silent hallways and upward through a warren of little rooms. He shows me some arches and stone walls dating back over eight hundred years. These, he explains, once belonged to a Benedictine monastery and now form part of the Catholic high school where he teaches and lives. As we climb a fourth flight of dark, squeaky stairs, he tells me, "Actually, we're climbing up here just to watch the sunset. St. Malo is famous for her sunsets, you know!" He leads me to a small closed window high above the western ramparts.

In the foreground beneath us the battlements, towers, and turrets loom in the lengthening shadows.

This would have been the hour when lanterns were hoisted high by ropes on pulleys to light the narrow streets. In medieval days the curfew bell, *la noguette*, was rung at ten p.m. and the town gates were shut tight. From the late sixteenth century through the eighteenth century, the streets were patrolled after dark by a unique police force: about fifty vicious mastiffs. These huge dogs that had been starved during the day were let out to roam the city streets after curfew and were recalled in early morning by the sound of a copper trumpet. In 1770, a poor sailor was coming home late and was caught by these canine "police." The grisly evidence was found scattered around the town next morning. Many an unlucky thief must have met swift justice this way over the centuries.

I'm pulled back into the present by the squawking of seagulls that wheel in graceful zigzags just outside our window. Beyond the dark ramparts, I can make out a ribbon of deserted sand and the gray line of a gentle soundless surf. Near the shore three rocky islets lurk in the shallow waves like beached sea monsters. Farther out in the bay, fiery flickers of setting sun dance on the silken wrinkles of the gulf of St. Malo. We watch in silence as the orange sun slips reverently below the horizon. Neither of us is willing to break the spell cast by the breathtaking beauty of this everyday event. I mutter a quiet, heartfelt prayer of thanks for the splendor of the spectacle I'm watching.

As a monk, I've been taught to cultivate a sense of awareness and of gratitude for the little things in life—a cool evening breeze, the rough texture of a sweater, the sparkle in a baby's eyes, or the bright face of a sophomore in the second row. How many times a day, though, do I pass by such gifts and not even notice them? Thanking God is more than just good manners; it is crucial to holiness. The more I thank the Lord for every little thing, the more I come to experience my dependence on God. The more I realize how much the Almighty has given me, the easier it is for me to trust in the Lord.

The custom of praying grace before and after meals is an important way of admitting that it is God who provides me with what I need.

By the same logic why not say grace before receiving other gifts as well? Grace before listening to Mozart? Grace before jumping into the pool on a hot day? Grace before opening the door to my cousin and her children who've come to visit? Grace at my desk before starting my daily job (thankful, perhaps, that I have a job to do)?

If I thank God after a meal because I recognize it as a gift, then why not a sincere grace after seeing the face of a particularly pretty girl? Or grace after a difficult but fruitful meeting? Grace after helping a slow student master a tricky French verb?

The saints believe that everything is a grace and a gift. Then why not say grace even on unpleasant occasions, in times of suffering, knowing that hidden inside of the pain is a mysterious gift from a loving God? Grace during an illness? Grace after a disagreement?

It's dark now, and Père Michel and I are still standing at our window. The gulls have gone home for the night. The sea is a rippling veil of black satin. The Bidouane tower broods over the ghostly ramparts below. Its pointed slate roof starts to tingle with the first flecks of silver as the moon comes up behind us. A silent prayer forms in my heart: *grace before moonrise . . .*

Being a Garden

The Channel Tunnel, England

08:09 a.m. *Ping-pong-ping!* The electronic chimes sound their warning. The shiny silver doors of the Eurostar train slide closed, and we roll smoothly out of Paris' Gare du Nord. On its second day of regular operation, the train smells of new carpeting and upholstery. Everything around me is sparkling and high-tech. This streamlined train, specially designed to run through the new tunnel under the English Channel, will whisk me to Waterloo Station, London, in three hours and six minutes. The sooty slate-blue of the November morning glides past my window as the train hums through suburban Paris.

08:20 We're now in high gear—186 miles an hour. The farm fields are pouring past like a river of pea soup.

09:36 An announcement in French and English warns us that in one minute we will be entering the Channel Tunnel. The automatic doors at the end of each car slide closed, and I begin watching for the tunnel entrance. A concrete wall starts running along the left side of the tracks, getting higher and higher. I glimpse a part of an arch that covers the tracks, like the corner of a giant's mouth. *Whoom!* We dive into the dark. I look out the big window and see nothing but my own neon-colored reflection in the glass. By shading my eyes against the light and leaning my head against the cold windowpane I can make out a dark brown-gray blur of wall. There won't be anything to see out there for twenty minutes.

09:57 Sunshine. *Welcome to Great Britain. Please turn your watches back one hour.* The constant high-pitched whistling sound that the train has been making in the tunnel disappears and the scenery takes up where it left off: rolling hills of green. Sheep graze under a clear blue sky. A strip of black road cuts under the railway, with two cars driving on the wrong side of the road.

09:28 (British time) Passing through Tonbridge, the first town since Paris to show me its name on a station platform. We are not moving as fast as we were in France, riding on old tracks laid through one of the most densely populated parts of the United Kingdom. In the Channel Tunnel train system, the British tracks are one of the problems still to be solved.

09:44 We slow to a crawl of maybe sixty miles an hour. We glide through Orpington, a town of brick houses and clotheslines that back up onto the tracks. We're still thirty minutes from Waterloo Station.

09:50 We've stopped. From high up on our embankment we look down onto row houses and a gasworks.

09:51 We start rolling very gently, as if this science-fiction machine is picking its way carefully among the backyards. Sunshine is bathing the forty-four empty seats—there are only twelve passengers in the car on this almost-maiden voyage.

10:00 We stop for the second time. It seems odd to be sitting on top of a railway embankment in this sleek futuristic cabin looking down into the narrow wintry backyards of brick row houses. An old man in a gray tweed cap is spading up his garden patch not a hundred feet away. Rich, brown soil, probably nourished with kitchen scraps and lawn clippings.

I'm struck by the contrast between the leisurely pace of the garden and the headlong rush of my high-speed train. The old gardener patiently turns under last summer's stubble to prepare the soil for the winter. Then he'll wait for spring planting time and then wait for the seeds to sprout. Then he'll gently nurture and weed and water his vegetables—and patiently wait for them to ripen.

This train, on the other hand, is designed to cover the greatest distance in the least possible time, delivering passengers efficiently and without ceremony from one city to another. If you're looking out your window and can still tell the color of the flowers along a fence or see the smile of a child as she waves at the train, you should complain that it's moving too slowly. For it to actually stop on the tracks like this is simply an unthinkable outrage.

It occurs to me that when I set to work at something, I'm a lot like this streamlined train: efficient and effective, zipping along my gleaming tracks as fast as I can go. Heaven help anyone or anything that gets in the way.

The man in the tweed cap stops his digging a moment and rests his crossed forearms on top of the spade handle. He squints up at the gleaming metal cars and stares at the twenty-first century, which has just expired up here on the tracks. He is looking right at me. His glance cuts through the window and touches me like an icy finger. A moment later, he turns back to his gardening.

If my life is like this speedy Eurostar, then being on this sabbatical year is sort of like being stalled on the tracks. I'm able to pause and look at myself. This morning an old gentleman and his little garden are challenging me to examine my approach to life. He moves slowly, while I rush around at 186 miles an hour. He spends most of his time waiting patiently—for spring thaw, for seeds to sprout, for tomatoes to ripen. I spend all my energy trying to make things happen on or ahead of schedule and according to my specifications. He works gently within the limits of the situation—a tiny patch of land, a given kind of soil, a certain amount of sunshine, his own decreasing strength. I fight my limits on every side—squeezing more minutes into one hour, reaching beyond the bounds of my own physical and mental energy, refusing to accept that certain things are just the way they are . . .

10:08 The Eurostar begins laboring forward at walking speed. We tiptoe through the tiny suburban station of Kent House, with tarmac platforms closing in on both sides.

10:14 We're now late. *Ping-ping-pong!* "Ladies and gentlemen, due to certain difficulties, we will be traveling at a slower speed than usual. We are sorry for any inconvenience this may cause."

10:17 We leave the residential suburban scene and jump into a dark tunnel where we pick up some speed. I wonder what the engineer's thinking right now as he gazes at his flickering computer screen. The Eurostar travels so fast that visual train signals along the track become useless blurs, so the engineer has to rely on a computer screen for all his information.

I have to admit that sometimes I start zipping along so fast that I can't see any of the warning lights, and I miss important signals about slowing down for my own good or for the sake of others around me.

10:20 Out of the short tunnel . . . Sydenham Hill station . . . Herne Hill . . . apartment buildings and row houses . . . worn-out neighborhoods of brick and asphalt . . . rough, shuddering tracks . . . A double-decker bus below . . . a wide river alongside—probably the Thames.

I think about the little man in the gray hat, and a snatch of Scripture from the prophet Jeremiah comes to mind. Speaking of God's chosen ones, the saints, the prophet says, "they will be like a well-watered garden." What if I were less like a speeding train and more like a watered garden?

If I were a garden, my efforts at prayer or work would take on a different meaning: anything that a garden "produces" comes as a *gift* of nature's bounty, a beautiful mystery. If I were like a garden, my notion of control would be completely different, because a garden can't be pushed or hurried along. A garden is to be tended, but not forced, not controlled, not driven headlong down some track like a train. If my life were a garden, then it would be a place of calm, patient waiting, where everything comes in its own due time: seasons of blossoms, seasons of plenty, and seasons of winter rain and seeming sterility. If I thought of my brother monks and my students as so many well-watered gardens, I would certainly approach them with more patience and gentleness and a more nurturing spirit.

10:33 *Ping-pong-ping!* The triumphant announcement that we're arriving at Waterloo Station, London. . . . *Sorry for any problems caused by the delay.* My ticket says, "Arrival Waterloo Int 10:13." We're pulling in at 10:35.

Being twenty-two minutes late really matters if you are an express train, but it's not so important if you're a well-watered garden.

PLAZA MAYOR - SALAMANCA

Part Five
Saints in Action

Paris

Saint Vincent de Paul

Rue de Sevres, Paris

Number 95, rue de Sevres, is a charming rabbit warren of buildings. Since 1817 it has been the mother house of *Les Pères de la Mission* (the Vincentians), founded in 1625 by St. Vincent de Paul. The Order has since spread around the world, bringing the Good News to the poor. Vincentians of all ages come and go in the hallways, speaking French, Spanish, English, or any of a number of other languages. Many are here for one of the ongoing refresher courses in the Vincentian charism and theology.

Vincent was born in 1581 into a peasant family in a village of southwestern France. As a young priest, he arrived in Paris and became chaplain to the rich and influential Gondi family. At the deathbed of a peasant on the estate of these nobles he became aware of the misery of the peasants. From this point on he began to actively organize help for the poor and the sick, and to preach missions to the simple folk on the Gondi estates.

Today, the mother house's unremarkable gray facade hides some pleasant secrets from the pedestrians walking by. Many of the rooms have recently been renovated, and the spacious garden area offers the opportunity for a quiet stroll among flowers and trees. At one end of the building is the sober church built in 1827. Above the high altar is a beautiful silver casket containing the remains of the saint, transferred from Notre Dame de Paris in 1830 . . .

Vincent's works of generosity expanded beyond the Gondi estate to reach the poor in the entire countryside and then eventually in the cities as well. In 1633, with Louise de Marillac, Vincent founded the Daughters of Charity. He composed their rule and gave them conferences as they became more and more invaluable collaborators with him in helping orphans, the sick, and the hungry . . .

In a hallway not far from the porter's desk hangs a large map of the city of Paris. Small red dots are sprinkled evenly over its entire surface. Reading the legend at the bottom I see that each dot marks a place in Paris that was somehow touched by St. Vincent during his life: an orphanage founded, starving people fed, a hospital staffed with sisters, a retreat preached, a school begun. There are dozens of these dots, each one telling a story of charity, of boundless energy, of commitment to spreading God's love on earth.

Vincent de Paul was not a profound thinker; he had no great original ideas. Yet few people have ever accomplished as much with their lives. His success was due to his great natural abilities, of course, and to a staggering capacity for work. But as I stare at the old map, I begin to realize that these dots are actually the fallout of Vincent's *spiritual* life. I can hear him insisting in one of his conferences, "You must start by establishing the kingdom of God in yourself first, and only then in other people." I hear him advising the members of his order, "You have to aim at the interior life, and if you're missing that, you're missing everything." He was always aware of God's presence when trying to help the poor, when agonizing over a difficult decision, or when suffering from the slanderous accusations of jealous enemies.

His intense prayer life had a surprising result: instead of becoming a visionary lost in the clouds of contemplation, he became a man of deeds. Vincent believed in the "indispensable priority of action." He didn't move from principles to practice or from insight to deeds; he simply began with love. This is the key to understanding his tremendous ability to get things done.

I find myself full of religious thoughts, pious ideas, and abstract principles that need to be applied. But of course much of this spiritual theorizing never finds its way into practice, into changing my way of living. Vincent's formula was simple: Start with love. Love is both a guiding principle and an action.

Vincent's great works for the poor were not his reason for existing—God was. He didn't go around giving his life to the poor—he gave it to God. Because Vincent de Paul knew he was loved by God, he could love God in return, and could cover this map of Paris with all these lovely dots.

The universal call to holiness is a call to a life of love. Each of us is expected to leave a bunch of red dots sprinkled across the map of our own life, marking places where our love has made a difference, made God's love real for others. I start to wonder what my own map looks like . . .

I hear a door open at the other end of the long corridor and see my Vincentian friend coming down the hall to greet me. I turn away from the map with a quick prayer to Saint Vincent that I might, like him, leave a little bit of divine fallout on the map when I die.

L'Abbé Pierre

Esteville, France

My friend Bernard and his wife, Colette, and I, are heading across the flat green farmland of Normandy toward an obscure village by the name of Esteville. Little pointed church steeples play hide-and-seek behind the distant rows of trees as we drive.

We are about to drop in unannounced on one of the best known and most venerated people in all of France, l'Abbé Pierre. Although this Catholic priest is famous in France and Europe, he's practically unknown to Americans, so Bernard has to spend the time filling me in as he drives . . .

In the early 1950s, Father Pierre Grouès, a young diocesan priest, opened his house to several homeless men. He called his group the "Emmaus Community." In order to support themselves, they began picking over Paris's city dumps and selling what they found to junk dealers. They used their surplus income to buy large vacant lots and build simple houses on them for homeless families.

In January of 1954, Abbé Pierre was deeply touched by the plight of the homeless men and women he saw sleeping on the sidewalks of Paris in the sub-freezing cold. When he realized that no one was doing anything for these people, he, poor as he himself was, began driving into Paris every night with food for those who were cold and hungry and forgotten. As the weeks of unusual cold continued he put up huge tents in vacant lots in the center of Paris to serve as shelters.

We're passing through a farming village. The sturdy silent farm folk look like characters from Guy de Maupassant's short stories. A road sign points to the town of Totes—this is the land of Madame Bovary . . .

In that same January of 1954, a woman froze to death in a Paris street, still clutching in her hand the eviction notice that had put her out of her little apartment and into the winter night to die. When Abbé Pierre told this story in church the next morning, the parishioners insisted that the rest of the country needed to hear about the horrible plight of France's homeless. So he prepared an address for broadcast on the radio and, with his incredible powers of persuasion, actually got a courageous radio official to preempt regular programming and allow him to deliver his plea. Up until that time, Abbé Pierre and his Emmaus brothers had been almost alone in the fight to help the homeless. This obscure priest had been living with the poor, encouraging them, bringing them a sense of dignity and of being loved, and had been building houses for homeless families.

That night on the radio, his straightforward statement of the problem and his impassioned appeal for everyone's immediate help pricked France's conscience. Some say it actually gave France back her soul. The plea, broadcast nationally, caused an immediate outpouring of good will from old and young, rich and poor, in every part of the country, but especially in Paris. As an afterthought, the young priest added a request to Parisians to bring their gifts and their help to a certain hotel just off the Champs Elysées. Within half an hour there was a traffic jam for blocks on every side of the hotel, as good-hearted Parisians brought hundreds of warm coats, sweaters and blankets, and thousands of francs in cash.

Abbé Pierre started delivering more radio addresses and talks that roused the nation's sense of social responsibility and, in fact, changed France's attitude toward the problems of the poor and the homeless. Over the next forty years, he would become the voice of the voiceless in France, acting as the country's conscience in debates on social legislation. To this day, polls show that Frenchmen still consider him the most trustworthy public figure in the nation. This is the man I'm about to meet . . .

Bernard pulls to the side of the road and stops to consult the map. Ulysse, the family poodle, sticks his nose into the map, too, and, tilting his head to one side, seems to study the route carefully. The car windows remain closed against the brisk autumn air. Through them, I see a couple of rugged stone farmhouses squatting nearby . . .

Although retired now because of age and failing health, Abbé Pierre has hardly been silent. In fact, a few weeks ago in the midst of the French presidential campaign and the debate over the economic implications of the new European Economic Union he posed a question to the conscience of Frenchmen. *"Et les autres?"* he asked publicly—"And what about the others?" Once again, the Abbé was speaking up on behalf of the poor and the forgotten . . .

We drive a few kilometers farther and then stop to ask a young woman for Abbé Pierre's house. We quickly find the nondescript, rambling collection of old brick farm buildings loafing, as if tired, beside the road. A tiny hand-painted "Emmaus" sign marks the driveway. As we pull into the bumpy parking area in back, I decide that the simple place seems just right for Abbé Pierre and his ragpickers.

The next thing I know, I'm standing in an enclosed courtyard shaking hands with a pleasant old man with a white beard and a navy blue beret. Abbé Pierre's slow gait hardly matches his bright, alert eyes and his quick, kindly smile.

Bernard, who is also meeting him for the first time, introduces himself and his wife. He then presents me as an American Benedictine whose monastery in the center of Newark, New Jersey, runs a school that welcomes poor children. The old priest nods in understanding and asks if I know a certain friend of his who works with the homeless in Harlem.

We chat easily for a minute or two. Instead of radiating a sense of energy or strength Abbé Pierre is surrounded by an aura of serenity—he is a man at peace with himself.

Then, not wanting to wear out our welcome, I kneel down and ask him for his blessing. After he finishes blessing me and I've stood up again, he says to me, "And now, Father, your blessing, please!"

A moment later we're back in the car driving away. Bernard is so overwhelmed he can't even speak, so we just ride in silence for some time, thinking about what we've just experienced . . .

What is the secret of this little man's great success? I ask myself. Part of it, certainly, is his effective use of mass media and his flair for the dramatic word or gesture. But lots of people have that. There must be something else. I think of a recent political cartoon in a French newspaper that concerned Abbé Pierre's forcing the French presidential candidates to take a stand on such social issues as poverty and low-cost housing: it shows the two major candidates wearing false beards and berets, each masquerading as Abbé Pierre, while the real Abbé looks on. The caption says simply "Beware of imitations!" This suggests the most important reason for his success: Abbé Pierre is clearly *the real thing.* He opened his house to homeless derelicts and misfits, gathering them into a community where they could find love and self-respect. He then set them to work putting up rudimentary housing for working people who couldn't afford a place to live. So when, in the winter of 1954, he spoke up spontaneously and sincerely on behalf of the homeless, his voice had a compelling ring of truth and authority about it because he had been living with the poor and devoting his whole life to them.

And now, his fifty years of living and working with the indigent have given him a license to speak up whenever the state or its citizens start forgetting their duty toward the homeless. And people pay attention. Abbé Pierre has *moral authority*—a priceless thing for anyone who wants to preach the Gospel. It doesn't seem all that complicated: he simply lives what he teaches. By being an actual flesh and blood example of Christ's love for the poor, he challenges a whole nation of Christians to live out their own call to Gospel holiness.

As we drive back past the lush green pasture land, I wonder about myself: how much moral authority do I have when I encourage others to sainthood? Does my way of treating people give me the authority to challenge my students to lives of selfless love? Does my way of responding to parishioners give a ring of truth to my Sunday sermons when I call people to endless, Christlike patience?

Abbé Pierre has just given me more than his blessing, he's given me a challenge: to make my preaching of the Gospel believable by living it first myself.

Assisi

Saint Francis

Assisi, Italy

A mile and a half of wet, black road stretches in front of me like a shiny sword pointing to the medieval hilltop town ahead. Menacing gray clouds swirl low over the flat farmland beneath Assisi. The thirty-minute walk takes me alongside furrowed fields that sleep in the chilly drizzle and dream of sunshine and clear summer skies . . .

In 1203 Francis Bernadone, the son of a cloth merchant, known for his high-spirited and worldly ways, suddenly renounced all of his possessions and his former life in order to take the Gospel literally. With no intention at all of founding a religious order, Francis soon attracted like-minded men to his new way of living the Gospel. The rest of his short life (he died at 44) was a marvelous mixture of joyful poverty, prayer, preaching, and suffering both physical and spiritual. An extraordinary young noblewoman of Assisi, Clare, was inspired by his vision and became his follower and friend, ultimately founding an order of women based on Francis's principles . . .

The town on the high hillside keeps getting closer. At its very top, the old fort sits like a retired soldier—sodden, sad, and obsolete. I can see the medieval town walls halfway up the slope, slicing across the face of the hill. Within five minutes, I'm through the fortified town gate and walking around inside old Assisi. The guidebook makes a fuss over the basilicas built to honor St. Francis and his spiritual sister, St. Clare. These churches are lovely, of course, but what really captivates me is the old town itself, which dates from the time of the two saints.

I wander through a maze of narrow streets connected by steep stairways. Cobblestone alleys wind between shuttered stone houses, beside terraces and beneath retaining walls. The medieval roadways, glowing silver in the drizzle, are barely wide enough for the little European cars that scuttle up and down the hill. I find myself standing in front of a building whose ground floor is now a small oratory. This, a sign tells me, is the site of the cloth-merchant establishment run by Francis's father. The living quarters upstairs are where the future saint was born and raised.

It takes very little imagination to picture the youthful Francesco and his friends strolling these same steep streets singing and carousing and keeping an eye out for the young ladies. I can hear the jangle of swords and armor, and the clatter of horses' hooves as a band of warriors thunders out of the town gate to join in the almost constant warfare against one neighboring city or another . . .

Under my dripping umbrella, I weave my way across the face of the hillside through streets and alleys and up flights of slippery stone steps, meeting only an occasional hardy tourist. February isn't a bad time to see Assisi, I think to myself, if you like to be alone!

I stop for a few moments at the edge of a terrace that overlooks the valley. Far below, in the gray distance, lies the tiny train station and, farther still, the overly solemn silhouette of Santa Maria degli Angeli which houses Francis's little Portiuncula chapel. In the foreground, just beneath me at the foot of a sloped retaining wall, lies a soggy little garden patch asleep in the winter rain. Near the outer edge of its narrow terrace is a small tree about ten feet tall. It doesn't seem to be a fruit tree as far as I can see. Maybe a nut tree?

Ah! Maybe it's the almond tree! I say to myself. I smile as I remember the story from the collection of charming legends called the *Fioretti*, edifying tall tales about the deeds of the wonder-worker Francis. On a winter's day, the legend has it, Francis stopped in front of a bare almond tree and said, "Sister almond tree, speak to me of God!" And with that, the almond tree burst into a mass of lovely blossoms.

He was already in the habit of letting the creatures of nature or the events of daily life teach him about God. This was his way of praying constantly, of staying in touch with God in every waking moment. So when the saint saw a bleak bare tree shivering in the drizzle, he just naturally asked it to speak to him of God. And in response, the Lord let the tree speak eloquently to Francis about God's fruitful, joyous, and overflowing love for the world.

How often do I let my surroundings speak to me of God? Do I ever look at a bleak situation or a deep disappointment the way Francis would have, expecting it to speak to me of God? Do I ever respond to a piece of bad news by inviting it to "speak to me of God"? When my carefully laid plans go awry, do I automatically ask the calamity to speak a word to me about God's care and concern for me?

The winter rain is thumping on my umbrella and cascading down the streets. Cool water is now seeping into my shoes . . .

"Speak to me of God!" Isn't it the job of every Christian saint to do that for other people? For better or for worse, we tell one another about God all the time without even realizing it. We speak about God without opening our mouth, by a compassionate smile, a conscientiously prepared class, or a thoughtful gesture to a stranger in a crowded supermarket aisle. What are the chances that by watching me a person can learn that God is love? Do my actions with my fellow workers speak to them of a God who is infinitely patient and slow to anger? Has a student in trouble ever walked out of my office after a talk with me saying to himself, "How beautiful God must be!"

My fingers are cold and numb from holding the umbrella. I shiver as I think what a bad impression of God some folks have gotten because of my indifference or impatience! On the other hand I console myself with what I have learned about God over the years from other saints: countless brothers and sisters, friends and family members. Their acts of patience and forgiveness speak to me of God and say, *Even if you're not always what you could be, God is always compassionate and kind, slow to anger and rich in mercy!*

My feet are now soaking. Time to find a place to dry out for a while. As I take a last look at the stark, black tree scratching against the gray sky I promise myself to return one day under a warm summer sun—to see if that little tree has almonds.

Footwashers

El Bosque, Bolivia

Night is falling fast as our taxi turns off the busy main road on the outskirts of Santa Cruz, Bolivia. We begin to bounce past dark patches of semitropical woods where cinder block shacks huddle together in groups as if looking for moral support. In the front seat, next to the driver, sits a Brazilian catechist. I'm in the back with a seminarian who has volunteered to come out here and help me celebrate the Holy Thursday mass. I've never been the chief celebrant on Holy Thursday—but at least I have said mass in Spanish three times before.

We jolt to a stop at the edge of a large grassy field with a whitewashed building in its center. Mass kit in hand, I climb out of the cab and tramp through the high grass toward the mission chapel of El Bosque, the taxi's headlights throwing long eerie shadows ahead of me. The large rectangular cinder block room with a metal roof and a cement floor is aglow with fluorescent lights. The Bolivian sisters who live and work in El Bosque and some parishioners greet us at the wide doorway. I can see over their shoulders the portable altar and long wooden benches arranged for mass. About two dozen people are already waiting patiently for the service to start. A couple of friendly dogs wander among the benches, but no one pays any attention to them. The seminarian starts to unpack the mass articles while I go sit on a bench in a far corner to hear confessions.

After twenty minutes the benches are full, and I walk over to the altar and vest for mass. The Holy Thursday eucharist begins with joyful singing accompanied by an electric keyboard, a drum, and a few guitars.

Soon it's time for me to read the Gospel. Today's passage is from the thirteenth chapter of Saint John, in which Jesus washes the disciples' feet at the Last Supper, telling them, "If I, then, the Lord and Master, have washed your feet, you must wash each other's feet. I have given you an example so that you may copy what I have done to you."

Later in the mass, I will perform the Holy Thursday rite of footwashing. Since the 1956 liturgical revisions, the priest presiding at the Holy Thursday mass dramatizes the gospel story of Jesus' action at the Last Supper by washing the feet of twelve people from the congregation who represent the apostles.

The earliest Christians included footwashing in the first baptismal rite and also used it as a ritual for welcoming guests into their homes. Caesarius of Arles, a sixth-century bishop, said in a Holy Thursday sermon how sorry he was to see Christians abandoning the custom of washing one another's feet . . .

The reading of the Gospel is finished, and one of the sisters begins a lovely reflection on the significance of Holy Thursday and Jesus' message of love . . .

At about the same time that Bishop Caesarius was lamenting the death of the Christian custom of footwashing, St. Benedict was preserving it for future generations in his *Rule for Monks*. In one chapter he calls for the weekly table servers to wash the feet of all the monks, and in another he orders the abbot and the brethren to wash the feet of the monastery's guests. Thus the ritual of footwashing would be kept alive over the centuries by the monks.

During the Middle Ages, the Benedictines continued washing each other's feet, but not those of their guests. The latter custom was replaced by a new one—the washing of the feet of poor people. Under the influence of this example, Christian kings and nobles performed this ritual gesture toward the poor once a year. In some medieval abbeys Holy Thursday was celebrated with as many as *three* different footwashing rites on the one day . . .

The sister has finished her biblical reflection. Wooden benches are set out in front of the altar, and the people who have been designated begin coming up to sit down and have the priest wash their feet. I remove my chasuble now and approach the first man on the bench, a wiry old *campesino*. I kneel down and wash his feet. It's not as strange a feeling as I thought it would be—maybe it's in my Benedictine blood? I finish drying the old man's feet and stand up to move to the next person.

When I glance down the long line of twelve people, I blink in surprise. At the other end of the row, the catechist is on his knees washing someone's feet, and in the center the sister is washing someone else's. *What*, I ask myself, *are these two people up to?* In a second, I understand what's happening. For the past few years there has been no priest here on Holy Thursday, and the catechist and the sister, the two central figures in this little faith community, have run the service themselves, including in it the footwashing ritual. I guess they and the community found it so meaningful and so beautiful that the two of them just naturally continued the tradition this year.

With three of us involved, the ceremony goes quickly, and soon I'm rinsing my hands and putting my chasuble on again to continue the rest of the mass. During the lengthy "General Intercessions" I notice my two fellow footwashers in the front row. I reflect on what the three of us have just done.

I, the visiting priest, was "playing Christ" in a liturgical drama by washing the feet of some people. But the other two were obeying the command of Jesus: "If I have washed your feet, you should wash one another's." I wonder if they realized that they were participating in a tradition that goes back to the first days of the Church. If Caesarius were here right now, he'd be nodding his approval.

A further thought strikes me: what the two of them do for people every day is a far greater lesson in loving service than the symbolic gesture they've just performed. The young Brazilian man gives himself entirely to evangelizing the poor and helping them solve all sorts of everyday problems. The Bolivian sister spends her days distributing medicine at the dispensary, working with children, comforting the dying, consoling the sorrowful, and bringing the Good News to the poor and the forgotten. These two saints give their lives for others, they become bread for their sisters and brothers by obeying Jesus' "new command" to "love one another just as I have loved you." This evening, their ritual gesture of service is a symbol of what they in fact do every day.

What if I had the vision to see each person in my life as someone whose feet I'm supposed to wash? What if my first response at the approach of a student, a brother monk, or a parishioner were always the desire to be of service the way Jesus was?

The seminarian brings the microphone over so I can pray the oration at the end of the petitions. This calls me back with a jolt as I look at the Spanish text in front of me and begin to read the prayer. As the congregation responds with their "Amen," I look out at all the saints on the benches. Some of them are barefoot, some in shower clogs. Many are wearing tee shirts and cheap cotton shorts. Their clothes tell a tale of poverty. But their faces say something else. Thanks to the catechist, the sisters, and others like them, these poor people know they are saints: they have experienced being loved by God, a God who kneels to serve them—a God who washes their feet.

Lérins "Abbaye Fortifiée"

Freshwater Monks

Lérins, France

The monks' white-and-blue boat is a sturdy little converted fishing craft. Perched on a hard bench inside its bare cabin, I watch through spray-spattered windows as the city of Cannes rolls and pitches, fading into the morning mist.

The choppy sea tosses our boat in three directions at once. I quickly learn from my two fellow passengers how to prop my feet and elbows to keep from being suddenly launched through a window and into the whitecaps. Now that I'm properly braced I can take my mind off of simple survival and think about where I'm heading. The monastery of Lérins on the island of St. Honorat is a very special place for me as a monk . . .

Except for a brief period after the French Revolution, St. Honorat has been a monks' island for almost 1600 years. About the year A.D. 400, a certain Honoratus arrived with a few companions in search of a secluded place in which to practice a new, experimental form of Christian life called monasticism. They settled on the snake-infested wilderness islet called Lerina and turned it into one of the great centers of monastic life in Europe. The successors of Honoratus renamed the island in his name, and tended it lovingly into a garden spot. Here they wrote some of the earliest monastic "Rules" in the West (St. Benedict wouldn't be born for another eighty years) and trained missionaries for England and Ireland (including St. Benedict Biscop and perhaps even St. Patrick). Their community provided many holy bishops for the cities of Gaul—most notably Honoratus himself and a special favorite of mine, St. Caesarius of Arles . . .

Careful to hold on to the wooden bench with both hands, I twist around to look out the front window. There it is, a tiny, tree-covered island lying low against the pink and tan clouds of the Mediterranean sunrise . . .

About the year 490 Caesarius, by now Bishop of Arles, wrote in a sermon to his brethren back on the island:

O happy isle of Lerina, which, while seeming small and flat to the eye, has nevertheless lifted countless mountain peaks toward the sky. It is she who forms eminent monks and provides such remarkable bishops to all the provinces.

I'm very conscious of this sense of tradition as I step off the boat in the quiet cove and begin a half-mile walk to the monastery of Lérins. The dirt road takes me past a stone hermit chapel, between hushed fields where scrubby lavender bushes rest in neat rows, then past quiet workshops and outbuildings. I remember that it was the monks of Lérins who developed a concept new to Western monastic thinking—the importance of manual labor. Earlier monastic founders in Europe such as Martin of Tours would not allow their monks to work at all so that they could be free to pray constantly. But on Lérins the monks believed in the ideal of a balance between work and prayer. As I walk past the island's well-tended gardens, fields, and vineyards, it's clear that the tradition is still flourishing today. I finally reach the monastery buildings. The whole island breathes an air of peace and of welcome, but this is especially true of the Cistercian monks themselves, who greet me warmly and make me feel at home right away . . .

St. Honorat Island is only about 800 yards long and 500 yards wide, and it takes less than forty-five minutes to follow its shoreline in a complete circle. During one such walk the next afternoon, I notice its larger sister-island, St. Catherine, across a narrow channel, and remember why the early monks had chosen the present island instead of the larger one. The explanation I heard that morning was that, on the mainland, far up in the hills behind Cannes, is a river. As it makes its way toward the sea, this river disappears underground, flowing under the mountains, beneath the shoreline, and below the seabed itself. It crosses under the Bay of Cannes, bypassing St. Catherine but flowing beneath St. Honorat before emptying its fresh water somewhere farther out in the Mediterranean. What had made the monks choose the little island over its larger partner, then, was its supply of fresh water. The underground river provided "sweet water flowing amid the bitterness of the sea." It was this that had allowed the monks to turn their rocky islet into a fruitful garden . . .

The next morning I stand outside the monastery, watching the sun rise over the pink spray of the waves that splash on the rocks. We've been up for a couple of hours. The gentle daily routine begins at 3:30 a.m. with Vigils and continues through periods of quiet and community prayer, reading, meals, and work in the vineyard, the library, the kitchen, or one of the workshops. But St. Honorat has not always been this peaceful . . .

Near one of the ancient hermit chapels, researchers recently discovered a *martyrium*, the burial place of several monks killed during one of the frequent raids in the early days. And out on a rocky point nearby, past the *martyrium* and the seaside chapel, a strange granite box of a building stares outward across the waves. It seems that the Saracens had a habit of raiding the island periodically over the centuries. The solution was this unique windowless stone cube, a four-story fortified monastery! Although the monastery-fort was abandoned quite a while ago, the bad times didn't end with the Saracens. In more recent years, the island monks have had to put up with cannons being placed on top of their hermit chapels and having troops billeted on their sacred soil.

But throughout all of these trials, the underground river kept flowing. When the gardens ran red with the blood of brothers slain by marauders, the river still ran clean. When the abbot had to travel to Spain to ransom two of his novices from the Saracens, the river still flowed fresh. When the ancient stone walls of a sacred hermit chapel collapsed under the weight of the clumsy cannon squatting on its roof, the hidden river still ran cool.

The life of every baptized Christian is like this islet in some way. We all have this spiritual river flowing deep beneath our everyday existence, giving us life, making us fruitful and beautiful. Under the surface of daily jobs and friendships, business and relaxation, the river of God's life, God's love, God's grace flows to make all of these things bear fruit.

The call to holiness is a call to stay in touch with this living water. Sometimes the well collapses through neglect, or it gets overgrown with shrubs and weeds until we can't find it. Sometimes in the heat of the day, we get so thirsty we forget that the well exists and we sit there cursing our desert island.

In that same sermon St. Caesarius, perhaps remembering the cool water of the underground river, writes to the monks of his beloved Lerina:

> *See, I am preparing the reservoir of my heart to receive*
> *the divine waters which flow through you. For I really*
> *know you well, and it is about you that we read this word*
> *of the Savior, "He who believes in me, rivers of living wa-*
> *ter will flow from his breast." . . . We joyfully believe that*
> *living waters flow from you like spiritual fountains . . .*

When we stay in touch with that faithful stream, when we keep drinking from that well of eternal life, then we are truly saints, sources of life for those around us . . .

The bell for Lauds is wafting across the island, borne on the crisp January sea wind. As I hurry to prayers, I pass an empty garden patch and notice how bare the soil looks. I'm comforted, though, by the image of the life that is flowing deep beneath the island at this very moment in the hidden, changeless river.

Child-bearers

Piray River, Bolivia

"Are you waiting for a lift across the river?" asks Father Roger in his British-flavored Spanish.

"¡Si, Padre! Gracias!" the young man answers as he steps toward the rear door of our four-wheel-drive. I suppose that he's been sitting beside the two-rut track here for a couple of hours.

I'm riding in the front seat next to Fr. Roger, looking ahead through the dusty windshield at the boiling brown froth of the river that lies between us and the low greenery on the other bank. Several broad sand bars split the Piray into a dozen wide channels of unknown depth. We're on our way to a village outside of Santa Cruz in central Bolivia to see the newly reconditioned church that dates back to the time of the first Jesuit missionaries. Once you leave the main highway, there's no paved road to this village. What's worse, it's on the other side of the river—and there's no bridge.

During the past few weeks in the rectory of the English-speaking missionary priests of the St. James Society, I've heard a few casual stories of one or another driver starting to ford some angry river and then getting carried off by the current. One such mishap had befallen a missionary not too long ago as he, his vehicle, and his passengers got washed down river. "He was okay, though. Wound up on a sandbar twenty yards downstream. I had to go out in the four-wheel-drive with the winch on front and pull him out," the narrator had said over dessert. River crossings attempted during very high water can end much more tragically, though. Everything depends on how high the river is.

Our young passenger perches on one of the two bench seats that face each other just behind me, and the padre shifts into first gear. With visions of river water sloshing in onto my ankles I lift my knapsack off the floor, trying to be casual about it. I sneak a glance between my feet to check for articles that may float away when the water starts spurting through the doors.

"Well, here we go!" our driver announces cheerfully, as we lurch down the muddy track that gives way to the sandy slope of the riverbank. The first of the swift, coffee-colored strips of river lies right in front of us, and we plunge straight into it, in what seems to me a great act of faith. I ask myself, *How does he know that this channel won't turn out to be six feet deep?*

Now we're completely surrounded by the muddy water, rocking along up to our non-existent hubcaps at a pretty good clip. Once I get used to it, it's sort of thrilling—just like in those articles I used to read as a kid in *Maryknoll Magazine*. I look out my side window and watch the foamy water sliding by. As I stare down into the ripples beside me, I'm hypnotized, and all sense of time and distance disappears . . .

". . . he had been a missionary down here for several years by that time." Father Roger, almost shouting to be heard over the rumble of the engine, has begun a story. I've missed some of it already. He continues, "The river had been rising for several days, and the padre figured he'd never be able to drive across. It was 'first penance' day for the children in the mission church out here, and the catechists had the kids all excited about making their first confession. So he decides to drive out on the slim chance that he'll find the river passable. He turns off the highway and comes down the same road we just did. He meets a fellow along the way who gives him the bad news—no chance of driving across that afternoon. The kids will just have to wait for another day . . ."

Whoosh! The wheels on the left side slump into a shallow dip in the river bed and my stomach jumps. Father Roger doesn't seem to notice, though, and goes right on with his tale as we crawl up onto a low sandbar and then plunge into the next channel . . .

"But the padre figures he's come this far so he may as well go on anyway and have a look at the river for himself. He continues on the road until he comes around that last bend right down by the river. Would you like to guess what he saw?"

Swoosh! We list sickeningly again, this time to my side. I stare wide-eyed at the bottom of the door, but all is still dry . . .

"Well, sure enough," continues the unperturbed Englishman behind the wheel, "the water was indeed very high—too high to drive through. But there, lined up along the road on his side of the river, were all the children, dressed up and waiting for their first confession! The parents had seen that the ford was too deep to drive across but they didn't want their children to miss their first penance. So the fathers picked up their children and put them on their shoulders and carried them through the water to the priest's side of the river. And there they were, all ready for him when he got there . . ."

Now we're sliding up the opposite bank, all four wheels churning in the loose sand until we're onto the bumpy ruts of another mud track through the scruffy shrubbery and ragged trees. The relative safety of the jolting ride on solid ground soon lulls me into thinking about those fathers on that afternoon a few years ago . . .

So many sincere parents give their families so much—in the way of material things. Those poor Bolivians couldn't give their children video games or electronic toys, dancing lessons or Little League baseball. Many probably couldn't offer them an education, or electricity in the house, or even decent drinking water. But they were able to give them the most meaningful gift a Christian parent can give a child— a God who loves us and forgives us. When the rising river threatened to keep the priest from getting to their church, the saints decided that if God couldn't get to their children, then they'd have to bring the children to God. So, across the ford they came that afternoon, laughing and shouting, wading through hip-high water, feeling for footholds, all the time carrying on their shoulders their sons and daughters, bringing them to meet the God of compassion.

I wonder what those little Bolivian boys and girls learned about God that day when their fathers lifted them onto their shoulders and delivered them across the seething river? I know they learned something about being a Christian parent . . .

A few houses start peeking out from behind the low trees now, and a wide clearing appears up ahead . . .

By the end of life's journey, a saint's shoulders ought to be aching with the effort of bringing others to meet the Lord through kind deeds, courageous example, and life-giving words of encouragement. More than once, I've had the experience of being lifted up and carried by someone right to the feet of the God of Mercy. On one occasion, I had to go to a brother and admit that a careless mistake of mine had just ruined the electric typewriter I'd borrowed from him. His gentle response gave me an unforgettable lesson, a sense of what God's forgiveness must be like. Do I ever do that for people who come to me to apologize?

From now on, when I meet someone in need of forgiveness, maybe I'll remember the example of those determined parent-saints who hoisted their little ones on their shoulders and carried them across the river.

"That's it up ahead there, on the left!"

Father Roger is pointing out the old Jesuit mission church—the place that a whole class of children left behind to celebrate their first penance.

La Clerecia ~ Salamanca

Part Six
Saints With Open Arms

Perpignan

My Fellow Citizens
Ciudad del Este, Paraguay

The bus floats noisily on the sluggish stream of traffic and exhaust fumes. A few minutes after crossing the bridge from Brazil into Ciudad del Este, Paraguay, we come to a stop near the Paraguayan Immigration Office. My three fellow passengers and I get off the bus and meekly follow our driver into a dingy office where a uniformed man is slumped behind a cluttered desk. While his thick fingers crinkle the pages of my passport he slurs an incomprehensible question at me in Spanish. After months of traveling in foreign countries, I've found that the best solution to the problem of the incomprehensible question is simply to give an immediate and confident answer of some kind. So I nod and reply in Spanish that I've just visited the Iguazu Falls and am on my way back to Bolivia via Asunción, Paraguay. He likes this answer—I wonder what the question was?—and shoos me on my way with a friendly toss of my thoroughly thumbed passport.

We climb back on board and drive to the nearby bus terminal to pick up about twenty-five more passengers. Soon the almost-full bus finds the busy two-lane road that will take us all the way across Paraguay to Asuncion. I settle into my seat next to a window for the five-hour ride . . .

In the past three days of visiting the breathtaking Cataracts of Iguazu, I've been in Argentina, Brazil, and Paraguay, bringing to fifteen the number of countries I've visited in my sabbatical travels. As comfortable as I am traveling in strange new places, wherever I go, I'm always conscious of being an outsider, of being "different." People seem to be able to spot me from a mile away as a foreigner.

Once, for instance, after browsing for some minutes in a little souvenir shop in Brussels, I walked up to the counter and the saleswoman said, in English, "You are an American of course." I exploded in fairly voluble French, "But I haven't said a word! How do you know I'm American, *madame*?" She couldn't explain it—she just knew, that's all.

And then there were those vendors selling little packets of sugar-coated peanuts in the parks of Paris. They prided themselves on spotting me at a hundred meters. As I approached one of those little carts its owner would ask smugly in bad English, "A beeg bahg or a leetle bahg, sir?" I always answered in French, "*Un p'tit, s'il vous plaît!*" How did they know I'm an American? Was it the way I walk? Or maybe the way I wear my clothes?

A French woman who had studied for years in London and spoke fine British English heard me make an announcement at a multilingual mass at Mont Saint Michel. She said to me afterward, "I love the way you pronounce English! I could listen to it all day! Say some sentences for me!" Even if Londoners don't share her enthusiasm for my quaint American accent, people who hear me speaking English certainly can tell where I come from.

We're out of Ciudad del Este now. On both sides of the highway runs a wide swath that includes a dirt service road, strips of weeds, scraggly trees, and sometimes a bus stop shelter or a tumbledown snack bar. Along the outermost edge on either side a variety of buildings face toward the traffic. A flashy new Toyota salesroom sits uneasily beside a car repair shop of unpainted wood with a dirt floor . . .

Different nationality groups do have certain characteristics that are more or less typical. A certain Italian bus driver comes to mind. He pulls to a stop at this traffic light on the route into Florence. He looks both ways to make sure no cars are coming, then drives merrily through the red light and across the highway.

In Cologne, Germany, the pedestrians arrange themselves in a neat row on either side of me, their toes at the edge of the curb. The people facing us on the opposite side of the street do the same. We are waiting for the traffic light to change. No one moves until the signal says to walk. Don't even *think* about crossing against the light!

In Asuncion, the capital of Paraguay, a stroll around downtown reveals only about four traffic lights. Drivers there just work it out among themselves without the help of red lights at intersections.

Traveling from one country to the next for some months has helped me to appreciate the remarkable variety that exists among various cultures and peoples.

We're now well out in the *campo*, the countryside. Cows and burros graze in the grass and gravel beside the road. Little children pad around in the red dust in front of pink or lavender one-room houses that face the highway in sets of four. Fountain-bursts of ragged palm leaves gush out of the ground without benefit of tree trunks. Slender pines make strange partners for the squat palms . . .

We seem to take on the characteristics of our homeland. I remember a phrase from a second-century biographer named Ennodius, who describes a local priest this way: "There was the outstanding priest, Bonosus, as celebrated for his holiness as for his noble bloodline, a Gaul by family origin but a native of heaven." Actually, all of us are natives of heaven. That's the only true homeland of the saints.

I gaze out of the smudged window at the volcano-shaped mounds of red earth beside the road—anthills as tall as a man—and I think . . .

What would happen if I began to act like the saint I'm called to be, like a native of heaven? I'd probably speak with a recognizable "foreign accent." People would know by my speech that I'm from somewhere else. The tones of kindness and patience in my voice would give my identity away. "Aha!" they'd say, "I know where *you're* from!"

Wouldn't it be great if from a hundred yards away others could pick up those unseen cues that tell them my real country of origin? If I carried myself with charity, trust, and humility, people would be able to recognize me as "an American by birth but a native of heaven." If I spoke comfortably about death or about God, folks would figure out that I'm "not from around here . . ."

We crunch onto the dirt service road and pull to a stop in front of a Japanese pharmacy that sits beside the road next to a Japanese store-restaurant in the middle of nowhere. An oriental couple climb aboard, and we roar off, leaving billows of dust and smoke.

The sun is sinking behind clumps of blue clouds that float on the watery orange sky. A young boy on horseback rides like a ghostly shadow among the slender trunks of tall palms, their shaggy heads silhouetted black against the sleepy sunset.

It's just about dark now in central Paraguay. Shouldn't I be feeling lonely or sad or at least ill at ease? After all, I am alone in a strange land, thousands of miles from home. But I don't feel like a foreigner this evening. No, right now I sense that I'm a fellow citizen of everyone on the bus. Our passports say we're from different countries, but we're all, like the saintly priest Bonosus, natives of heaven . . .

I flick off the dim reading lamp and peer out into the darkness. On the horizon is the first faint glow of the lights of Asuncion.

Be Where You Are
Amsterdam, Holland

A young mother plods across the snow-covered bridge, tugging a tiny sled made entirely of wood. On it sits a rosy-cheeked child in a blue snowsuit, holding on with both mittens. I pick my way carefully along the narrow icy sidewalk that runs beside Amsterdam's Prinsegracht canal. The white cover of snow glistens in the January sun, a startling contrast to the jet black water . . .

In the seventeenth century, when Holland was one of the great commercial powers of the world, Amsterdam's merchants built the canals that give the city her unique character. On the narrow streets alongside each canal they built endless rows of stately brick houses that peer down into the water today . . .

In this particular neighborhood, the waterfront buildings are more modest, and some have small businesses on their ground floors. I arrive in front of number 263 Prinsegracht . . .

At the time of the Nazi invasion of Holland, this was a factory and warehouse belonging to a Mr. Kugler, a dealer in spices. Two of his employees, Herman van Pels and Otto Frank, were Jews. During the worst days of the German occupation, when Jews were being hunted down and deported to death camps, Kugler let his two employees hide with their families in a secret set of rooms in the back of his warehouse.

Among the eight people in hiding was Frank's daughter, Anne, a bright and sensitive girl who had just turned thirteen when they entered the annex. During two years of hiding she kept a diary which was found and published after her death. This book, *The Diary of a Young Girl*, has touched the hearts of millions of readers throughout the world, and has made number 263 Prinsegracht into a shrine.

There is nothing to distinguish the building from the others on the block: its narrow brick facade is taken up almost entirely by large windows that stare wide-eyed at the street and the canal. I stamp the snow off my boots and climb several steps into a very simple lobby where I pay the admission charge for a visit to "The Anne Frank House."

A couple of other visitors climb a narrow wooden stairway with me to the second floor. The old stairs protest noisily, creaking under our feet. On the landing at the top, I see the bookcase that swung on hinges to conceal the secret stairs leading to the hidden rooms in back. The first room beyond it, now bare of furniture, is the Franks' living room where Mr. and Mrs. Frank slept. Next to it is Anne's cubicle which she'd decorated with pictures of movie stars. Some of the yellowed clippings are still on the wall just as she describes them. Excerpts from her diary are posted in appropriate places in the different rooms. There has been no attempt to re-create the place with substitute furniture. Nor is there any need to—the empty rooms are alive with the sad, courageous spirits of the frightened people who hid here for two years. Having read Anne's diary myself, I feel I know them all.

There is Mr. Frank, who understands his daughter, and Mrs. Frank, who doesn't. There is their other daughter, Margot. Quiet, easygoing, and docile, she's the opposite of her sister, Anne. Then there are Mr. and Mrs. Van Pels (called the Van Daans in the diary) and their son, sixteen-year-old Peter, whose friendship eventually "makes all the difference" for Anne. A dentist, Fritz Pfeffer (in her diary she calls him Mr. Dussel), shares a little room with Anne.

The spirit of the owner, Mr. Kugler, is here, too, along with those of his employees Miep and Jan Gies and other selfless people. These good Christians risked their own lives every day in order to support the eight fugitives. For two years they were the only source of food and supplies, local news, and much-needed encouragement.

The person whose presence I sense most of all, of course, is Anne—sensitive, passionate, insightful, courageous, and optimistic. The recent complete and unexpurgated edition of her diary shows her to be, in addition, a headstrong and self-centered teenager given to normal outbursts of immaturity and moodiness. She had hoped to be a writer some day.

As I climb the steps to the top floor which doubled as kitchen and as the Van Pels' bedroom, I start to realize that there is also another presence in these rooms, something both subtle and overwhelming at the same time. It is the sinister sense of evil that floats through the whole place like some poisonous haze. Anne Frank's hideout is crowded with millions of ghosts: not only the Jews of the Holocaust, but every victim of Central American death squads, every Black lynched by Klansmen in the middle of the night, every political prisoner ever kidnapped and tortured, every woman and child victim of genocide in Rwanda and the former Yugoslavia . . .

Downstairs, fists begin pounding on the secret door—the one hidden behind the bookcase. Rifle butts and Gestapo boots crash through the thin wood and into the hiding place. It is August 4, 1944. All eight of the occupants are quickly dragged off to concentration camps at Auschwitz or Bergen-Belsen. The young girl's diaries are left scattered on the floor. Miep Gies will gather them up the next day and put them away for safekeeping, unread.

Anne Frank will die in Bergen-Belsen, three months short of her sixteenth birthday—just weeks before the Allies arrive to liberate the camp. Her mother and sister will die, too. Only Otto Frank will survive . . .

Weighed down with pessimism about the future of humanity I work my way through the last tiny room and follow the tour arrows down some stairs. In the small ground-floor museum, there are several displays about present-day racism and political repression. Large placards hold quotations from Anne's diary. One of them seems particularly poignant under the circumstances:

> *In spite of everything, I still believe that people are really good at heart. If I look up to the heavens, I think that this will all come right, that this cruelty too will end, and that peace and tranquillity will return again.*

Schoolchildren and a few families are milling around in the small exhibit area and crowding up to the book counter. I glance at the stark, heartrending exhibits for a few minutes. I'm not sure whether to be uplifted by Anne's courageous spirit or depressed by the power of the hatred that killed her. Finally depression wins—I've had about all I can take for one day.

The cold, damp air blowing across the Prinsegracht bites into my cheeks as I step outside. I wrap my scarf over my mouth and nose and set off through the frozen streets with a heavy heart. My walk soon brings me back toward the crowded center of town where streetcars and bicycles spatter through the slush in the cloudy gray afternoon. Squat, sturdy boats rumble mournfully about their business on the icy ink of the Heerengracht canal.

I'm snapped out of my gloomy thoughts by an unexpected splash of color off to my left. A poster-sized photograph is sparkling in the window of a bus tour company: bright yellow tulips stretch endlessly across a field beneath a clear blue sky. Alongside the picture are the dates and prices for the spring tours of tulip fields that are still buried in snow this afternoon. I step close to the plate glass window for a better look. It's a lovely picture: acres of tulips glowing in the warm spring sunshine, inviting me to come and join them.

I stand still for a few moments trying to put myself into the photograph. I try to feel the warm breeze on my face and the sun on my back. I try to smell the rich aroma of the moist, fertile soil and touch the velvet petals of the spring flowers. But it just doesn't work. I seem stuck here on this side of the window.

Becoming a saint requires a constant commitment to being right where you are. It means embracing the pain of a difficult or depressing situation with open arms as your unique way into the mysterious suffering heart of God. This afternoon, the Lord of Love is not looking for me in that meadow of Easter flowers, but on this slushy sidewalk. The voice of the One who died and rose is speaking to me not from the glorious empty tomb, but from the ominous empty rooms of the Anne Frank House.

My hands are getting cold, so I stuff them deep into my jacket pockets. I turn a bit wistfully from the tulip field and continue crunching my way carefully down the icy sidewalk.

Saints and Statistics

Santa Cruz, Bolivia

She is barefoot, wearing the common dress of Bolivian Indian women, with underskirts that puff out to make her look unnaturally heavy in the hips. Her jet black braids disappear over her shoulders and down her back. The young mother is just greeting us when her husband comes trotting up from somewhere across the dusty lot to join the group. Their house, really just a shed, is one of several strewn about among the low tropical shrubs and scrawny trees. It's a slab of concrete with wooden walls and a corrugated metal roof. The couple lead us solemnly into their home. The single room has windows only in the front wall next to the door, so that even on this mild autumn day in May, it's hot inside. Two twin beds shoved together take up half of the entire place. The family's belongings fit onto a few shelves next to the wheelbarrow that's leaning against a wall. There's no plumbing to be seen. No stove. The three-year-old girl I've been carrying squirms out of my arms and runs off past her parents and out the door. Her dirty white dress is the same one she had on at the 7:00 mass last night. I was concelebrating with Father Joe, an English diocesan priest newly arrived in Bolivia . . .

It's time for the "Sign of Peace," and the two of us walk out into the wide airy nave to exchange a handshake and a greeting with the seventy-five or so people. It's also a chance to bless the little babies and make a fuss over the toddlers. Toward the rear of the church stands a dark-skinned Indian couple, their dress and their faces give them away as simple country people, *campesinos*. Probably from up in the Andes near LaPaz. I'd noticed them filing in late, the mother sober and preoccupied, the father carrying the baby wrapped in a white blanket. I come up to him and shake his hand as he carefully switches his bundle to his other arm. To see the infant, I slowly lift back a corner of the baby blanket, noticing the pattern of flowers—little pink and blue ones. A shiny dark eye sparkles up at me. I gently touch the baby's cheek with the knuckle of my first finger. Then as I lift my hand in a blessing an old woman's voice rasps in a loud stage whisper "*Está muerte, padre. Tiene que baptisarlo.*" My hand stops in mid-blessing as the words hit home, "He's

149

dead, Father. You have to baptize him." I stare down at the tiny face again and realize to my horror that the glistening eye is in fact not moving or blinking. It is frozen there like a bead of black glass. I feel as if the earth has just gaped open under my feet. In a daze, I mechanically replace the corner of the blanket over the dead baby's face and tell the parents to wait until after mass. I return to the altar in a stunned trance . . .

To the left of the twin beds, the small white casket is propped on a table. A couple of neighbors have squeezed into the small room to pray with the heartbroken parents whose faces are haggard with grief and shock. Fr. Jim, a Bolivian sister, and I have come to celebrate the "funeral." According to Bolivian custom, the funeral will be just a simple prayer service at home before the body is taken to the cemetery. The masses will come later, on the anniversaries of one week, one month, six months, and a year.

The priest sprinkles holy water and says an opening prayer in the stuffy room. Sister begins a Scripture Reading. "We want you to be quite certain, brothers, about those who have fallen asleep, to make sure that you do not grieve for them, as others who have no hope . . ." I watch the mother standing near me. The sharp, almost craggy features of her young face are contorted in pain. That's the way she looked last night when they brought the dead baby straight from the hospital to mass to ask us to baptize him . . .

In the back pews of church after the mass, a group of curious onlookers joins the family and friends in the impromptu prayers for the baby. The priest explains that the child doesn't need to be baptized, that he's already with God, but that we can pray together and give him a blessing. "What is the baby's name?" he asks. "His name is Juan Domingo," the mother whispers. Then she begins to pour out her tragic story to the sympathetic ear of Father Joe.

Just this morning, a newspaper article gave some grim statistics about the quality of life in the State of Santa Cruz. As the woman tells her tragic story in a soft, half- choking voice, the newspaper's cold statements and abstract numbers seem to answer her like the mocking chorus of a Greek tragedy.

"My baby had terrible diarrhea." "*The most common cause of death in children in Latin America is dehydration due to simple diarrhea.*"

"We had no doctor to go to, but finally we brought him in to the hospital in town." "*34% have no health services available to them.*"

"The first thing the doctor said to me when he looked at my son was 'This baby is dirty!'" "*45% have no running water, but rely on wells, pumps and tanks.*"

"When I told him that my son had very bad diarrhea, the doctor scolded me. He shouted, 'Why do you feed your children water that has not been boiled first?'" *"47% lack access to basic sanitation."*

"He died in the hospital soon after we brought him there. My little son! My little son!" Now I hear a response with an American accent: *"Well, in third world countries life is cheap. And babies there are always dying, so people are used to it."* Someone, I think to myself, ought to come and tell this mother that she's supposed to be used to it. She looks as heartbroken as any grieving mother I've ever seen in the United States . . .

Sister has finished the reading, and Father is preaching a simple sermon about trusting in God even in the face of mysterious tragedies. Everyone is listening intently to his simple words, hoping to glean a bit of consolation from them. It's very still in here. You can hear the flies buzzing. There's a short litany, and some final prayers for the baby and for his devastated family. Then a parting blessing for baby Juan Domingo in his little white casket.

As we step outside into the cool fresh air everyone is offered a drink of some dubious-looking white liquid from a plastic pitcher. The Bolivian sister accepts with a grateful smile, but I decline as gracefully as I can. Father Jim explains to our hosts that Padre Alberto has a "Gringo stomach" and cannot accept the drink. Everyone nods knowingly and sympathetically. "Ah yes! Of course! The poor visiting padre has *estómago de Gringo!*" The parents understand my breach of etiquette, and express their thanks to us for coming. To have two priests and a sister at their little son's funeral was a great honor.

The three of us whisper sad good-byes and leave the family and the silent neighbors to their tears. We climb into our rugged vehicle for the bone-jarring ride back along the dirt track. After leaving Sister off at her convent nearby, we turn toward the center of the city. Along the main highway that leads downtown a billboard advertises the new five-star hotel.

Soon my weeks in Bolivia will be over and I'll be back in the United States. The reality of the "third world" will quickly fade into a vague memory, a series of interesting color snapshots in an album. I will still feel as helpless as ever in the face of so much poverty and suffering in the world when I return and start teaching school . . .

An inner voice interrupts my musings, *"48% of the population will never have a chance to go to school."* Last night's Greek chorus of statistics is starting again. Suddenly I realize that something has happened to me in the past twenty-four hours, something that has changed me forever. Now the statistics speak with a human voice—the haunting whisper of a heartbroken mother with black braids. Now the numbers have a face—a little brown one with a single black glassy eye staring up at me. Today, third world statistics have been given a name—Juan Domingo.

I am richer and more sensitive for having met him. Now Juan Domingo sleeps forever in my heart, cradled in his father's arms and wrapped in a white baby blanket with flowers on it—little pink and blue ones.

Falling Up

Chambord, France

We're standing on the vast lawn that lies in front of the chateau of Chambord. The fertile farmland of the Loire Valley, an hour's ride south of Paris, has always been considered well worth fighting over. During the Middle Ages, fortified castles—*châteaux*—sprang up all along the valley as various nobles tried to defend their claims to their domains. With the coming of gunpowder and cannons and the end of feudal warfare, these forts lost their military value and were converted into fashionable residences. Elegant windows were cut into their walls and lovely flower gardens laid out in their moats. The chateaux built later were never military buildings at all, but were designed from the start as splendid country residences. The most outrageous of the later kind of chateau is Chambord.

Even at this distance, well back from the building, it's hard to take in the whole thing in one glance. Three hundred and sixty-five chimneys and scores of spires and pinnacles float like an aerial village of gray slate above the colossal classical facade. On this side alone, there seem to be enough windows for most of the 440 rooms. This is the hunting lodge of King Francis the First, a triumph of playfulness and fantasy, and the first flowering of the Renaissance in France.

My friend Jean and I start to stroll around outside Chambord's vast bulk in the afternoon sun, overwhelmed by its size and charmed by the variety of its architectural surprises. Jean recognizes an old army friend, and they strike up an animated conversation. I wander a discreet distance away from them to watch the activity on the front lawn. A large hot-air balloon, glowing white and blue in the sunshine, is just lifting off. It glides slowly upward like a mysterious vision, a giant soap bubble swinging noiselessly over the chimneys of Chambord . . .

I think of little Kari, my friend's six-year-old back home, giving me a long account of her classroom birthday party. She told me that each child had been given a helium-filled balloon. I asked her, "What would happen if you let go of the string on your balloon?" She answered matter-of-factly. "Oh! It would fall up!"

As a creature held down by the heavy hand of gravity, I was fascinated at the time by the image of a thing dropping not toward the earth but toward the sky. There was something delightful about the notion of "falling up."

By nature, I tend to be focused and intense about everything I do: keeping deadlines, getting jobs done and getting them done well. My personal style seems to lean naturally toward heaviness. Now, far from my duties and obligations, I find myself asking, *What would happen if I let go of all that heaviness and lightened up in my approach to life?* Maybe I'd fall up . . .

The hot-air balloonists rising gently over the fantastic chimneys and towers of Chambord know a couple of the secrets of holiness.

First, they have a sense of perspective. From their vantage point, the balloon's passengers can see the whole chateau, the 55-square-kilometer wooded "park" of Chambord and the farmland beyond. Balloonists and saints have a sense of the real lay of the land. If I were to lighten up, maybe I'd be able to see my tasks and my troubles in their true proportions and not let them become more important than they really are.

Second, they know serenity. Neither the balloonist nor the saint is preoccupied with the future (neither of them knows exactly where the wind is going to take them!), but both are experts at savoring the present moment. If I responded to deadlines and the pressures of planning with the lightness and tranquillity of the balloonist, I'd probably be easier to live with. Would I also be less effective? Less efficient? Somehow, as I watch the calm gracefulness of the blue balloon, the words "effective" and "efficient" seem to lose their attraction for me. Instead I'm with the balloonists high overhead. I can feel the gentle breeze, and can laugh as I look down at the carefree play of pinnacles and gables on the chateau's roof below . . .

The great white tulip on the side of the balloon is growing orange as the afternoon sun settles on the tops of the trees. Jean has finished his long chat and is striding quickly down the path toward me with "apology" written all over his anxious face. I'll just tell him to lighten up a little.

Saints Without Walls

Berlin, Germany

Berlin's outdoor Christmas Market is in full swing. Scores of temporary wooden stalls line the crowded streets in the center of prosperous "West" Berlin, and shoppers wander slowly from one to the next looking at the leather goods, sweaters, neckties, wood carvings, handmade jewelry, and plastic toys. They line up two deep at long outdoor bars that serve bratwurst and beer, or they stand in groups talking and drinking hot mulled wine in front of stalls that advertise *Heisser Glühwein*. The city has a festive pre-Christmas atmosphere about it.

Reluctantly I turn from this scene to report for my guided tour of Berlin. Several other tourists are already on board the comfortable double-decker bus when I arrive. I settle in next to a window on the upper level and wait . . .

A tour of Berlin, more than of any other European city, is a quick trip through the history of the twentieth century. Berlin was intimately connected with the Prussia that was instrumental in unleashing World War I. She nurtured some of the most important movements in painting and literature. She witnessed the rise and fall of Adolph Hitler's Nazism, paying for it with her life's blood. She saw herself cut into two parts, like the world itself, by a wall that separated the Communist bloc from the "free world" of the West.

The bus rumbles into motion and the multilingual guide begins pointing out the important sights.

On your left is the main railroad station . . . Also coming up on your left is the War Memorial in the bombed-out ruins of the church called the Kaiser Kirche. It has been made into a shrine to pray for peace . . . On your right you can see the Christmas Market . . . Up ahead on your left is the city aquarium . . . Across from the aquarium, notice the high-priced hotels for expense-account travelers, and the modern glass towers that are home to dozens of multinational corporations...

There's a feeling of busyness and prosperity on every side.

Ladies and gentlemen, we are now approaching what was formerly the dividing line between "East Berlin" and "West Berlin." On your left you can see some remains of the Berlin

Wall, and the guard post called "Checkpoint Charlie." The wall was begun on August 13th, 1961, and was torn down on November 9th, 1989 . . .

The bus rolls silently past a ragged, graffiti-covered stretch of the wall that has been left standing as a reminder of the years the city spent artificially divided into "East" and "West" Berlin. This ugly relic still has a sinister aura about it.

We rumble toward a large sign that once inspired fear but is now merely a curiosity for tourists. The driver slows down and twenty cameras point out of the left-side windows to click at the white signboard that warns ominously: "ACHTUNG! ATTENTION! *You are now leaving the American-controlled sector of Berlin . . .*"

The bus rolls onward across the one-time border and into the former East Berlin. I'm shocked at the contrast. It's as if a color movie has just turned to black-and-white. The buildings are faceless, gray concrete cubes lined up along sad streets in monotonous rows. No anti-Communist propaganda film from the late fifties could do a better job of evoking the dismal mood of lifelessness and oppression.

That building on your right was the headquarters of the Soviet secret police. The one up ahead, on your left, is where political prisoners were taken for interrogation . . .

A large gloomy field lies strangled by high weeds—in the center of the city! For the first time today, I notice how dark the clouds are overhead, and how chilly it looks out there . . .

We will now descend from the bus for ten minutes so that you may take photographs of the Brandenburg Gate . . .

It's bitterly cold when I step out of the bus. I start sketching the gate but soon decide to climb back aboard and finish my work from the comfort of my warm seat by the window. The Brandenburg Gate fades in and out behind my breath condensing on the glass . . .

My mind keeps being drawn back to that ominous section of The Wall. If this bus tour is teaching me anything it's this: a wall that's meant to divide people is an ugly thing.

Some individuals have a wall inside with barbed wire on top, and have put whole groups on the other side of it because of their skin color or nationality or religion. Some of us, even ones who are striving to be holy, put up more subtle walls because of fear or insecurity or anger.

One of the great tragedies of the dividing of Berlin into "East" and "West" was that relatives who happened to be living at different ends of town in August of 1961 suddenly found themselves on opposite sides of a wall with no way of communicating with one another. The call to be human is the call to be sister or brother to everyone else on the planet. The Berlin Wall was a tragic parable in cinder block. It taught the world that any wall that cuts me off from another human being cuts me off from a member of my family.

Jesus set us the example when he ignored the walls that others had put up. He befriended women, lepers, prostitutes, tax-collectors, Samaritans, and other "outcasts" who were walled out of accepted society in his day. It is clear, then, that we saints need to be careful not to let Berlin Walls grow up inside of our own hearts. A wall can happen very easily, for lots of different reasons: anger, fear, jealousy, and so on.

I quietly cut myself off from a particular person because of some injury or insult, justifying my behavior with the knowledge that I am right and the other person is wrong. Then over time the division becomes a normal part of my life, as if it belongs there. I stop noticing how ugly it is. But whatever its reason for being, no matter if I am "right" or not, to the extent that this wall divides me from a brother or sister, it divides me from God, who always identifies with the person on the other side of the wall.

Newsreels show the delirious joy of the Germans on the day the wall came down. The symbol of their dividedness had crumbled and left them celebrating. What better invitation to all of the saints to join in breaking down the world's walls wherever we find them?

Ladies and gentlemen, we will now continue our tour with a ride down the famous avenue called Unter den Linden . . .

The linden trees are stark and bare in the dead of December. This whole part of the city looks as if it has been in the grip of winter for fifty years.

I promise myself to come back one day and visit Berlin in the summer. In the sunshine everything will look prettier—everything except The Wall.

Perpignan

Dancing With the Saints
Perpignan, France

The early summer evening is perfect for a stroll. I follow the carefully manicured banks of the canal that winds across the center of Perpignan, until I come to the Castillet. This grumpy fortified gate was built in 1370 and made into a fortress a century later. I take out my pad to do a quick sketch.

Catalonia spans the eastern end of the Pyrenees from Perpignan in France to Barcelona in Spain. Her people have a strong ethnic identity that comes from their common language called Catalan, their rich cultural heritage, and their proud history. The Castillet stands as a reminder of the glorious days when pugnacious kings sallied forth from stone fortresses to strike fear into the hearts of their enemies.

With my sketch pad back in my knapsack, I cross the canal and wander around the narrow streets of the oldest part of town. I pass a sign that reads "Sardane ce soir 20:00 h."—tonight the Sardana, the traditional folk dance of Catalonia, will be danced somewhere at eight. Finally I stop at a typical Catalonian cafe. I sit at a small sidewalk table and spear black olives and navy beans with a sturdy toothpick while studying the lively scene around me. From here I can see, about a block away, cafe tables crowded together into a semicircle under their bright blue umbrellas. They form the curved side of a large, open plaza. Along its straight side runs the high wall of the Castillet. Against this old stone building, a temporary platform has been set up with two rows of chairs on it.

As the daylight fades into evening I slowly work my way through the *parrilade de viande*—a selection of grilled Catalonian sausage, lamb, beef, and a pork chop. When pedestrians pass along the quiet sidewalk, I try to guess their life stories while I eat. I notice that down in the plaza a crowd has started to gather and a couple of men are sitting up on the platform holding trumpets. I smile at my good luck—I've accidentally discovered the place where they're going to dance the Sardana!

Suddenly, floodlights pour a golden glow onto the Castillet and the sense of expectation grows as people begin to line the edges of the plaza. By the time I finish up my *flan à la catalane*, twenty musicians in white open-necked shirts and black pants or skirts are warming up. There are clarinet-like woodwinds, trumpets, a bass violin, and a piccolo. After a tiny cup of black coffee, I pay my bill and edge toward the plaza to get a closer view.

Just as I arrive, the band launches into a pleasant, lively folk melody. Everyone listens appreciatively. A young woman, obviously the leader of the musicians, sets the tempo on a tiny drum the size and shape of a rolled up newspaper. Another warm-up tune is followed by a minute or two of rest. Then the leader gives three smart whacks on her drum: *tock! tock! tock!* The musicians launch into a leisurely, lilting air that is different from the first two. A few people leave their cafe tables and walk slowly out into the empty center of the cobblestone plaza. A couple from a different table joins them, and then another, until there are about twenty people holding hands in a circle. They dance the Sardana with hands held motionless at shoulder height, each dancer clasping the hand of the person on either side, men alternating with women. The circle doesn't rotate—everyone stays in place as their feet weave what seems to me an intricate set of steps. There are young people in the circle, but they're far outnumbered by those in their fifties and older. The tempo is very slow and relaxed at first. Then the beat starts to increase and the dancers' light feet begin speeding up to keep pace until the final crescendo when the dance comes to a sudden end. Everyone applauds as the dancers drift slowly back to their coffee cups and wine glasses. The musicians play another folk tune and then pause for a short rest.

Tock! tock! tock! The leader's drum starts the band off again in a slow, swinging Sardana gait. This time a few dozen people leave their chairs and come out into the plaza, spontaneously forming three circles, then four. Each group joins hands to make a motionless wreath of arms and shoulders that bobs slightly while feet draw deft, noiseless patterns on the paving stones.

In the wall of the Castillet, just above the gateway, is a niche containing a statue. A stone Virgin Mary, holding her baby, is looking down on the dance. I remember a medieval song called "My Dancing Day," in which Jesus, the leader of the dance, calls us all to join him:

> *In a manger laid and wrapped I was*
> *So very poor this was my chance*
> *Betwixt an ox and a silly old ass,*
> *To call my true love to the dance . . .*

These Sardana dancers seem proud of what they are doing. "This," they are saying to the watching tourists, *"this is us! We are proud of being Catalonians."* Another verse of the song comes to mind:

> *Before Pilate then was I brought*
> *Where Barabbas had deliverance;*
> *They scourged me and set me at naught,*
> *Judged me to die to lead the dance . . .*

There is a beautiful unity in a Sardana circle: old people and young, men and women, in dresses and in jeans. A pony-tailed man holds the hand of an older woman in a long skirt and a lovely silk blouse. These two have probably never met before, but here in the circle they are mysteriously united, sharing the same elegant steps. As I watch this scene, the last verse of the song comes to me. Jesus sings:

> *Then up to heaven I did ascend*
> *Where now I dwell in sure substance,*
> *On the right hand of God, that all*
> *May come unto the general dance . . .*

All at once the four circles become one big one, and all of us spectators around the plaza start to join in. No one misses a beat as more people keep hurrying onto the cobblestones and adding to the circle. Chinese people in subdued gray outfits join us, and Nigerian women with bright-colored head-wraps. The circle just keeps getting larger and larger. South Americans with faces like Inca carvings, and little children from Iraq and others from Israel are all holding hands in the one big circle.

All my brothers from the monastery arrive in their black habits. As if by magic, the Sardana has now reached far beyond the plaza, past the canal, and down across the river Têt. There are Eskimos and Australian aborigines, Bosnians and Serbs and Croats. And still they keep coming to join in the dance. Protestants from Belfast arrive to clasp hands in the circle with their Catholic neighbors. The line stretches out of sight in both directions. Everyone is dancing to the music with chins held high, as if to say, "This is *us!* We are one proud people!"

As I join the dance with my brothers and sisters in this single enormous circle my eyes fill with tears: I am holding hands with the whole world! A voice from inside says to me, "Yes! This is the way it *could* be. The way it *would* be if we were to let the Lord lead the dance." Then, to my amazement, my parents and grandparents who died years ago are there, too, hands held elegantly, their feet effortlessly going through the steps. The pace increases, and feet tap faster and faster. The ground itself is vibrating with the rhythm. This is the final crescendo . . .

Everyone is applauding, and the dancers are drifting back once more to their coffee cups and wine glasses. The cobblestones are empty as the band strikes up another interlude. It's time for me to leave to catch the midnight train for Rome. I stand and start off, all alone, on the one-mile walk to the station. There is a light Sardana bounce to my step . . .

Certainly the world has a long way to go, but every now and then we catch a preview of the General Dance. Whenever someone acts like a brother or sister to someone else, the world draws a step closer to its goal of unity. A little white child walks to school holding hands with her African-American classmate. All the Christians in a certain town put Chanukah lights in their windows as a sign of solidarity with a family victimized by anti-Semitic vandalism. Two warring factions in some troubled country agree to stop fighting and open peace negotiations. From the saints' point of view each of these is a preview of what is surely going to happen sooner or later. On that day, the Lord of the Dance will stand up and invite all the peoples of the world to join hands as brothers and sisters in a final Sardana. One great circle of dancers will embrace the whole earth and reach upward into the clouds of heaven. The Lord of the Dance, Jesus himself, will give the signal to start the General Dance—three smart raps on a little drum: *tock! tock! tock!*

Epilogue

I've been back in my monastery for some months now. Summer has long since turned into autumn and autumn into winter. As I close my venetian blinds, I notice Jack Frost's handiwork on my window—delicate crystal fern leaves pressed between the glass and the black velvet of the night. I set my alarm clock, switch off the bedside lamp and snuggle under the covers . . .

I'm riding a subway in Manhattan with some teachers from our school. I realize, though, that the car we're in is actually from the Paris métro. The feel of the French subway train brings back a flood of delightful memories: the Louvre, Sacré Coeur Basilica, the Seine. Soon the tracks shoot out of the dark tunnel and into a bright sunlit afternoon. We are rattling northward along a narrow spit of sand. Gentle waves roll onto a wide white beach to our right. On our left a sparkling bay lounges alongside the tracks, its far shore lined with low green hills. The scene reminds me of the Mediterranean coast above Perpignan.

Across the bay an ancient walled city sits sunning itself on a high hill. At its summit a lion-colored castle and a bizarre domed church elbow one another for position beneath the deep blue sky. They look strangely like Edinburgh Castle and Marseilles Cathedral. The stone walls might be Avila's, or maybe Toledo's. As we get closer to the town a familiar feeling comes over me—the urge to explore a strange new place. The questions I used to ask myself during last year's travels come back once again: What forgotten tales could those old buildings tell? What language do the people speak? What traditional dishes do their cooks brag about? My curiosity keeps growing as the train clatters into the station.

Something nudges my left knee. I look down and see my suitcase resting between my feet. That settles it! I jump up and ask my friends if anyone wants to come with me on a walk through this town. No one does. Promising to catch up with them later, I hurry down the aisle and step off the train just as the doors close. I'm watching the subway pull away when I realize that I've left my suitcase on board. There's nothing to worry about, though —I'm sure my friends will take good care of it for me. Then I turn and set off eagerly toward the maze of mysterious streets . . .

The alarm clock on my windowsill is splitting the monastic stillness with impatient peeps, like the nervous chirps of an electronic bird. It's four forty-five. I slide my feet out onto the cold floor, take one long step toward the clock, and silence it with a clumsy swat.

I start my brief morning routine of washing and dressing. As I go through the automatic ritual, I think about the dream I've just had.

I'm pleased with myself for deciding to get off the train and visit that town when I had the chance. I have the feeling that now I'll be able to go back and explore those streets whenever I want.

What could it mean that my fellow teachers and I were riding a Paris métro car from Manhattan into that intriguing town? The whole dream seems to be telling me that somehow I'm still on an exciting trip.

Of course! Come to think of it, I've been on a wonderfully interesting journey most of my life, right here in the monastery! Doesn't St. Benedict tell his monks at the beginning of his Rule that they are to spend their lives "on the road" together?

. . . as we progress in this way of life and in faith, we shall run on the path of God's commandments, our hearts overflowing with the inexpressible delight of love. Never swerving from his instructions, then, but faithfully observing his teaching in the monastery until death, we shall through patience share in the sufferings of Christ that we may deserve also to share in his kingdom.

Benedict could just as easily be speaking to every Christian on the road to sainthood when he uses this optimistic image: "See how the Lord in his love shows us the way of life. Clothed then with faith and the performance of good works, let us set out on this way, with the gospel for our guide, that we may deserve to see him who has called us to his kingdom . . ."

Dressed in my habit but still half asleep, I start down to the first floor to get a cup of coffee so I won't doze off during my meditation. On the stairs I remember that suitcase I left on the train in the dream—the same one I used on my sabbatical trip. Maybe it's telling me that there are a lot of things I've brought home with me but haven't "unpacked" yet, surprises that I'll keep discovering for the rest of my life.

There is one great gift from last year that I'm already aware of: the dozens of saints that came home with me, new companions on my life's journey. One or another of them is always showing up unexpectedly, usually just when I need his or her help.

If I'm getting uptight because some project isn't going exactly according to plan, a violist or the bass player from my support group in St. Julien le Pauvre will probably show up with a reminder: God doesn't expect saints to be perfect but rather to add to the world's harmony.

Although it happens less often now, there are still times when my life starts gathering speed like an express train. That's when the old London gardener in his tweed cap stops by. Leaning on his spade he simply raises an accusing eyebrow at me as if to ask "What's the big hurry?" That's usually all it takes to slow me down for a few days.

The other morning I was in my office in school girding for battle—a 9:00 meeting with a problem student and his angry father. Just then, two friends from Santa Cruz, the Brazilian catechist and the Bolivian sister, appeared. He put a large basin of warm water on the floor by my desk and Sister handed me two white towels for drying people's feet. "We thought you might be needing these this morning . . ."

The dim glow of a single light is spilling familiar shadows across the oak floor and long wooden tables of the dining room. The aroma of coffee floats on the air. I see a brother monk, a traveling companion of mine for over thirty years, standing in the corner by the coffeemaker. He's waiting patiently, mug in hand, for the morning's first pot to dribble out of the coffeemaker.

The monastery is stirring to life. The Lord is giving us one more day on the road together. Another brand-new chance for each of us—for all the saints—to just let go and watch what happens.